Warping Time

Warping Time

How Contending Political Forces Manipulate the Past, Present, and Future

Benjamin Ginsberg and Jennifer Bachner

University of Michigan Press
Ann Arbor

Published in the United States of America by the
University of Michigan Press
Printed and bound by CPI Group (UK) Ltd, Croydon, CR0 4YY
First published April 2023

A CIP catalog record for this book is available from the British Library.

Library of Congress Cataloging-in-Publication data has been applied for.

ISBN 978-0-472-07600-0 (hardcover : alk. paper)
ISBN 978-0-472-05600-2 (paper : alk. paper)
ISBN 978-0-472-90334-4 (OA)
DOI: https://doi.org/10.3998/mpub.11760539

The University of Michigan Press's open access publishing program is made
possible thanks to additional funding from the University of Michigan Office
of the Provost and the generous support of contributing libraries.

To Sandra and Daniel

Contents

Digital materials related to this title can be found on the Fulcrum platform via the following citable URL https://doi.org/10.3998/mpub.11760539

List of Tables

List of Figures

Preface

As social theorists have observed, control of time through dates, deadlines, and schedules is an important instrument of power.[1] Governments and other bureaucracies exercise power by compelling subjects and employees to adhere to official calendars and clocks while, for their part, dissidents endeavor to "rupture" such temporal hegemonies in order to undermine the power of the institutions that control them.[2] Generally speaking, those who seek to exercise power in this way do not actually manipulate the passage of time. Rather, they demarcate time's passage in ways they find useful without presuming to change time itself, in effect marking notches on the arrow of time as it moves inexorably along its course. We might call this practice temporal fine-tuning to distinguish it from the gross tuning of efforts to actually intercept the arrow and use it to reconstitute political reality.[3]

Most of us are, of course, familiar with the idea of the arrow of time in which past, present, and future follow a neat progression. In the political realm, however, the arrow of time twists and turns, doubles back on its tracks, gets stuck, and even shows evidence of heterotemporality, that is, simultaneous movement in more than one direction. The arrow of time, moreover, is not simply a natural phenomenon following its own laws and independent of social intervention. Instead, the arrow can be held in human quivers and wielded by humans for their own purposes. Norbert Elias and, more recently, Andrew Hom use the term "timing" to character-ize the instrumental use of time.[4]

The role of timing is quite evident in the history of history. The histori-cal past is seldom set in stone and, indeed, can be revised even when it **is** literally carved in stone. Take the destruction of pre-Muslim stone artifacts by the Taliban, or even the removal of Confederate monuments in the U.S. today. As we shall see, history is at least partly a result of human intervention, driven by interests and ideas and not the product of impersonal forces or material conditions. Humans are the architects of history, not its captives. By the same token, what we believe the future to hold is subject to constant revision, which, in turn, leads to changes in attitudes and behavior in the present. In these ways, much of what we know as political reality is politically determined.

And, while it may seem that only ideas and not physical objects can move backward as well as forward in time, this is not exactly true. Ideas about the future affect contemporary behavior including the construction of material objects in the present. Revision of ideas about the past, moreover, can lead to changes in behavior in the present and future. Ideas moving about in time may materialize anywhere or anywhen.

On the question of whether time exists apart from consciousness we take an intermediate position, informed by the work of philosopher/scientist Karen Barad.[5] Temporal reality, like material reality, is not exclusively a human construct, but neither is it independent of human consciousness. Reality, including temporality, is a product of the continual interaction between humans and other elements of nature. In essence, human observation and understanding of the past, present, and future interacts with physical phenomena in an ongoing constitution and reconstitution of reality.

One element of this interactive reconstruction of reality is human history. Individuals' understanding of the past is what Maurice Halbwachs termed "borrowed memory."[6] For the most part, recollection of the past is not a matter of personal observation. Memory is, rather, based upon what individuals are told by others or, more importantly, have learned from histories, films, and even novels. Memory is shared and collective and historical memory is the work of writers, filmmakers, and other historians. It is the mediated and collective character of historical memory that can make timing a powerful political tactic. Contending political forces engage in timing when they seek to rewrite the collective past to influence the present and shape the future. They also engage in timing by reimagining the collective future by developing narratives that are calculated to change contemporary ideas and behavior.

As Ronald Krebs and others have observed, the myriad facts of political life acquire meaning only when woven into coherent stories.[7] Hence, rival political forces often compete to develop powerful narratives that blend past, present, and future into cogent tales with which to shape political debates and action. Consider the following examples:

1. Between the 1870s and the 1960s, the history of Reconstruction in America was dominated by the "Dunning school," which emphasized the suffering of southern Whites at the hands of former slaves. This history was designed to justify and fortify America's system of racial segregation. Since the birth of the civil rights movement and the mobilization of progressive political forces, this history has been rewritten.

2. When the United States moved to enter World War II as an ally of Soviet Russia and foe of Nazi Germany, the Franklin Delano Roosevelt administration worked to revise Soviet history to erase Stalinist brutality and to emphasize the similarities between Americans and Russians. After the war and the beginning of the Cold War, Soviet brutality was rediscovered and the Germans, now American allies, were reimagined as good people who had been misled by the Nazis. Some wartime pro-Soviet films were actually recut and rereleased as anti-Soviet dramas.

3. To bolster support for Scottish independence, the Scottish National Party propagated a history of English brutality and aggression while imagining a glorious future for an independent Scotland. The nationalist party's historiography, however, overlooked the fact that England was, for centuries, ruled by Scottish kings and governed by Scottish prime ministers.

4. The dystopian French novel *Soumission* (*Submission*) imagines France under Muslim rule. The novel has served as a rallying cry for parties of the European right who demand action in the present to prevent this imagined future.

5. Israelis and Palestinians, along with Serbs and Croats and many others, have developed rival histories of victimization to justify brutal conduct in the present to produce a glorious future.

In the pages to follow, we consider the construction of a number of these temporal narratives. Beyond simply assessing the narratives for purpose and content, however, we undertake a series of quantitative experiments using an original survey to estimate the extent to which new narratives can actually affect respondents' beliefs about the past and future and, in turn, influence their political and policy preferences in the present. The survey was conducted using Qualtrics, a survey design and administration software platform. We surveyed a nationally representative sample of 1,814 respondents. Additional details about the survey are presented in chapter 2 and the complete survey instrument appears in the appendix.

In our first experiment we demonstrate that altering respondents' understanding of the past can have a marked effect upon their policy preferences in the present—in some instances so marked as to produce an erasure effect in which respondents seem to forget that they once held other views.

In our second and third experiments we show that presenting respondents with alternative forecasts of future conditions can change both their preferences in the present and their understanding of the past.

In our fourth experiment, we show that presenting respondents with politically congruent histories and forecasts—a tactic not infrequently used in the political world—can have a powerful impact upon respondents' preferences in the present.

To be sure, not all respondents were convinced by our efforts to teach them new histories or by our future forecasts. For some, established historical understandings were sticky and some respondents clung to their established preferences even when they accepted our histories and forecasts. We offer some observations about the sorts of persons more and less likely to remain temporal dissidents despite our efforts to teach them new facts.

In sum, we conclude that political reality and, in particular, temporality is uncertain, contingent, and subject to human manipulation. In the article cited above, Andrew Hom wrote that "timing is everything." We conclude, from our experimental evidence, that timing is not everything, but it is certainly something, indeed, something of importance.

CHAPTER I

Time and Politics

Political Time Travel

In a 2017 speech, Virginia governor Terry McAuliffe declared that the Confederate monuments should be removed because they helped to keep racism alive in present-day institutions and attitudes. President Donald Trump, for his part, argued that those attempting to remove the monuments were seeking to rewrite history in order to remove all traces of ideas with which they disagreed. Though they differed on the proper course of action, the two politicians seemed to agree that the power to describe the past is also a power that can alter present-day political realities. The monuments themselves functioned as what Pierre Nora has called *lieux de memoire*, or sites of memory, that help to symbolically fix or institutionalize a particular memory.[1]

This was certainly not an isolated incident. Throughout 2020, protestors across the United States sought the removal of Confederate monuments and the renaming of streets and buildings that memorialized slavery and slave owners. Since the list of American slave owners includes such giants of the American founding as George Washington and Thomas Jefferson, these demands called for a significant recasting of the history of America.

In this vein, the *New York Times* launched the 1619 Project. This project is an ambitious effort to "reframe the country's history by placing the consequences of slavery and the contributions of black Americans at the very center of our national narrative."[2] In other words, it casts aside the narrative most often taught in American K-12 schools that emphasizes the virtues of American civilization and nobility of American democracy.

Revision of the past in order to change the present and future is, of course, a standard science fiction theme. In one of the more memorable moments in recent popular film history, Arnold Schwarzenegger, portraying a murderous cyborg, or "Terminator," materializes in present-day Los Angeles surrounded by bolts of energy. The Terminator, we learn, was sent from the future, to win a war between humans and machines by killing the future human leader while he is still a child. While enthralled by the imagery, most viewers understand, of course, that the film is pure fantasy. Travel through time to win wars or change the outcomes of political struggles is impossible. Or, is it?

This is a study of the ways in which contending political forces actually manipulate time, rewriting the past to influence the present and future, reimagining the future to change the present, and reinventing the past to comport with and legitimate a desired future. These efforts, which we shall examine via narrative examples and original experiments using a special survey we designed for this book, summate to a kind of political time travel that can have important, and even surprising, consequences.

Social scientists, unlike most physicists, generally take a Newtonian view of time. They assume the existence of an objective past, similarly experienced by all observers, that can be discovered through historical and archaeological research. Historians, in particular, distinguish between the past and subjective memory of the past. Those social scientists who make use of time-series data, moreover, assume that events occur in temporal sequence, with a certain and immutable past followed by a definite present and a future that is a product of the past and present. Based upon this understanding, historical institutionalist and rational choice theorists, for example, emphasize "path dependency," that is, the idea that choices made in the past render some contemporary possibilities more and less likely, while choices made in the present affect future courses of action. Few, if any, social scientists entertain the idea of reverse paths and detours in which the past, present, and future are not so neatly arrayed.

The Newtonian paradigm is, however, not the only way to conceive time. The special theory of relativity, for example, holds that time is relative to the reference point of the observer. General relativity, for its part, posits that time can be dilated by velocity and gravity and opens the possibility of travel into the past and future. Quantum theory questions the unilinearity of time. Indeed, though much disputed, so-called delayed choice quantum eraser experiments have suggested that events in the present can change what occurred and was recorded in the past, calling into question the entire Newtonian understanding of past, present, and future. Even Albert Einstein, who was not enamored of some of the implications of quantum theory, reportedly observed that the past, present, and future are only illusions, even if stubborn ones.[3]

The creation, destruction, and re-creation of these illusions can be a powerful political tactic. Take the story of the past. An effectively infinite variety of macro and micro events took place in the past. History consists of those events of which we are aware and have collectively chosen to remember, along with often competing interpretations of their relationships and significance. History is not something that happened—it is a story written and rewritten by human authors. If they are able to rewrite history, governments and other political forces might change the loyalties and political preferences of millions of individuals in the present. And since, as Jeffrey Haydu observes, individuals use information about how problems were solved in the past to help them solve problems in the present, changing stories about past solutions can affect present-day approaches to problems.[4] Similarly, if they can change future expectations, political interests might alter the contemporary behavior of individuals and even nations. And note that political time travel involves not only the temporal transit of ideas. It can affect material objects, organizations, and institutions as well.

Perhaps only ideas, thoughts, memories, and interpretations can travel freely backward and forward in time. However, once they arrive at their destination, ideas are capable of materializing, as if to demonstrate the validity of Max Planck's well-known observation that matter is derivative from consciousness. New ideas about the past can influence the creation of political movements in the present to avenge past defeats or recapture past glory. Similarly, new ideas about the future often lead to physical action in the present to guard against supposed threats or to take advantage of imagined opportunities. Each year the United States spends billions of dollars on weapons systems on the basis of such future projections. Let us consider some of the implications of these ideas, beginning with the relationship between action in the past and action in the present.

Past and Present

If we view politics from a non-Newtonian perspective, past and present are not necessarily so distinct, nor are they neatly sequential. To begin with, mirroring special relativity theory, political history is certainly affected by the observer's frame of reference. Take the case of an international agreement such as the 2016 nuclear weapons agreement between the United States and Iran. It is hardly unusual for the several signatories of a treaty immediately to quarrel about the document's meaning. Each will have a different interpretation of the negotiations and discussions leading up to the treaty as well as the precise meaning of the treaty's words. Which interpretation is really correct? There is no single right answer—the answer is dependent upon the observer's frame of reference. All the relevant parties will have different understandings of what was said (and was meant, insinuated, implied, and so forth in the course of the negotiations). Subsequently, various parties are likely to interpret the treaty according to their own interests and perspectives.

Competing ideas about history have certainly surfaced in contemporary political battles in the United States. To some, for example, Hispanic and Latino immigrants arrived in the United States seeking safety and opportunity while others assert that these immigrants came to smuggle drugs and engage in criminal conduct. To some, Islam presents a history of peace and religiosity while, to others, Islam has always been associated with war and conquest. Which of these alternative historical ideas prevail in the political arena is likely to have important implications for policy choices waiting to be made in the present.

Peaceful and industrious immigrants surely deserve the promulgation of policies giving them a path to citizenship while the threat of criminal noncitizens might call for enhanced border security. History matters. Similarly, in France today, competing political forces offer alternative historical narratives to bolster their claims to power in the present. "History is war," declared one French journalist.[5] In a similar vein, several historians have suggested that current Chinese international policy cannot be understood without reference to China's understanding of its own history—an understanding that differs from American views of Chinese history.[6]

On this general point, historian Timothy Snyder cites the example of Polish and Ukrainian memories of the Second World War. For Poles, the Molotov-Ribbentrop pact of 1939, secretly dividing Poland into German and Russian zones, was an act of Russian treachery. For Ukrainians, the same pact united Ukrainian lands into a single unit and became the basis for a Ukrainian state.[7] Or take the recent case of battling cinema versions of events in Turkey during World War I. One 2017 film, *The Promise*, is a love story emphasizing the horrors of the Armenian genocide in which Turkish forces murdered more than one million Armenians during the early days of the war. A rival 2017 film, *The Ottoman Lieutenant*, is a love story set in the same region during the same period that depicts Turkish officers as behaving generously toward Armenians displaced by war and bloodshed.[8]

Recently, critics of Ken Burns's monumental documentary history of the Vietnam War, aired in eighteen parts by PBS, have asserted that the documentarian sought to rewrite and sanitize American history by depicting the war as having been "started in good faith by decent men." In fact, say critics, the war was a failed episode in American empire building. Rather than good faith, the war was a product of "self-interested geopolitical calculation and prejudice."[9]

And, of course, in 2022, Russian president Vladimir Putin, offering pretexts for Russia's invasion of Ukraine, asserted that Ukraine had always been part of Russia. Most Ukrainians rejected this assertion, but the periods of history when Ukraine *was* a part of Russia left enough room for Putin to exploit in justifying the present costs of war to the Russian people.

Each of these historical perspectives has its avid defenders who sift through events to produce a narrative proving their view to be correct. In effect, there are infinite pasts with the dominant interpretation of the past defined more by political struggle than historical research. And, of course, each interpretation has implications for the present day. Are those who make American foreign policy decent individuals capable of error or are they avaricious imperialists bent on global domination? If the first, the answer might be remonstrance while if the second the proper response might be resistance.

The above examples might be seen as metaphors for rather than actual examples of special relativity. But, if so, they reflect a Maxwellian use of metaphor or analogy—the great Victorian physicist James Maxwell termed it the "method of physical analogy"—as a mechanism to help explain a conception as clearly as possible by comparing phenomena that resemble one another in form.[10]

Some events, of course, seem to have a more tangible and sticky existence than others. If terrorists kill a prominent political figure, or destroy a building, that individual is dead and the building turned into rubble regardless of the observer's frame of reference. Indeed, the second law of thermodynamics probably forecloses the physical reversal of such events.[11] Yet the meaning and significance of any event is open to debate and interpretation and can change with time. Moreover, in time, memory of the event is likely to fade, particularly if important interests find that they have a stake in erasing it from the record. The event was real in its own present but may gradually slip out of existence in its future. As seventeenth-century political philosopher Thomas Hobbes put it, "After great distance of time, our imagination of the past is weak; and we lose . . . of actions, many particular circumstances."[12]

The fact that the observer's frame of reference affects political history points, in turn, to the possibility of quantum-like phenomena involving reverse temporal paths and detours from the Newtonian version of temporal reality as observers, and their frames of reference, change over time. For instance, events that occur in the present may affect understandings of the past, which may, in turn, work to alter both the present and future. Take the case of Reconstruction after the American Civil War. During the late nineteenth and early twentieth centuries most histories of Reconstruction emphasized the sufferings and struggles of southern Whites in the wake of the Civil War. This historical perspective sympathetic to southern Whites was presented in such works as the famous 1940 film *Gone with the Wind*, as well as by D. W. Griffith's 1915 silent-screen epic, *The Birth of a Nation*, which ends with the knights of the Ku Klux Klan riding to the rescue of a group of innocent Whites besieged by a band of former slaves, depicted as savages intent upon rape and murder. This latter film debuted in a special White House screening where it was received with great enthusiasm by President Woodrow Wilson. Wilson reportedly remarked, "It is like writing history with lightning, and my only regret is that it is all so terribly true."[13] When the film was shown to popular audiences it sparked a number of attacks by Whites upon Blacks throughout the nation.

Similarly, pre–World War II academic history and school texts, dominated by the so-called Dunning school, emphasized the unreadiness or incapacity of newly freed Blacks to exercise political rights and applauded the efforts of White southerners to reclaim their political supremacy in the region.[14] Generations of students learned a historical narrative that gave legitimacy to the South's apartheid system and to policies of racial discrimination in such realms as housing and employment.

Beginning in the 1950s and 1960s, though, this version of American history began to be inconsistent with changing conceptions of race relations and with a political agenda calling for greater racial equality. Accordingly, the older historical narrative came under attack by progressive political forces who properly saw it as blatantly racist and inaccurate. By the 1970s, the history of Reconstruction was being corrected to emphasize the many injustices visited upon Blacks by southern Whites in the aftermath of the Civil War. Tens of millions of Americans viewed *Roots*, a 1977 ABC television miniseries based upon a novel by Alex Haley that depicted the suffering of African Americans during slavery and Reconstruction. Most of the Whites portrayed in this film were villainous and it was the Ku Klux Klan members now depicted as murderous brutes.

Academic historians, for their part, strove to rewrite the textbook history of Reconstruction to emphasize the accomplishments of African Americans in the realm of politics and government until their abandonment by northern politicians and violent suppression by White southerners who stripped Blacks of voting rights. Even in today's South, the old history of Reconstruction is the history generally learned by schoolchildren today. As historian Eric Foner has noted, the old history of Reconstruction reflected and was designed to reinforce one set of political understandings, while the revised history was intended to comport with and reinforce contemporary understandings born during the civil rights era.[15] And, once a new set of memories becomes established, many individuals will begin to forget that they ever believed something different. This exemplifies a phenomenon that psychologist Daniel Kahneman calls "substitution."[16] In chapter 2, we shall analyze data from an original survey to show that substitution can have a powerful effect, not only changing individuals' memories of the past but even their memories of what they, themselves, previously thought.

How the Present Affects the Past

Does the modern-day revision of nineteenth-century history actually exemplify the past undergoing changes because of choices made in the present? After all, when Arnold Schwarzenegger's homicidal android stormed into its own past to change the future, its tactic was not literary revisionism but the physical erasure of a key individual. The Terminator aimed to alter facts, not interpretations and recollections.

Perhaps historical revisionists do not have the power of the Terminator to change the past before it happened so that particular events, facts, or individuals are simply eradicated. Yet, from their perch in the present, those seeking to revise history can amend the past in three important ways. They can, as we saw above, reinterpret the past, offering new explanations for accepted facts. Of course, events and facts derive much of their meaning and significance from interpretation. With reinterpretation, the events of Reconstruction took on new meaning for Americans. Second, historical revisionists can adduce new facts that will reshape the accepted historical narrative. Thus, modern historians of Reconstruction highlighted the legislative achievements of Black-led southern state governments, before Blacks were stripped of voting rights in the former Confederacy, to counter the prior view of Blacks being unable to lead in civil society. Third, historical revisionists can seek to becloud or conceal once-accepted facts, in effect obscuring or even erasing them from the record, if not from existence. For example, as historian Jill Lepore shows, modern day "Tea Party" Republicans rewrote the history of the American Revolution to comport with and reinforce their contemporary political views.[17] More recently, as seen above, the 1619 Project has sought to retell the story of America's founding to emphasize the centrality of slavery and racism.

In these ways, America's remembrance of the past has been revised—a revision that, in turn, had important consequences for the present. For example, proponents of the 1965 Voting Rights Act pointed to the previously ignored history of the violence used by southern Whites to deprive former slaves of their newly won political rights. This "recovered" history became the basis for the federal government's authorization to undertake special supervision of states and jurisdictions that had long discriminated against Black voters. Thus, a newly adduced historical fact helped to bring about a change in the present.

The importance of the past and, hence, struggles to define precisely what happened in the past appear, according to political theorist John Keane, to be most pronounced during periods of crisis. Keane writes that "crisis periods . . . prompt awareness of the crucial political importance of the past for the present. As a rule, crises are times during which the living do battle for the hearts, minds and souls of the dead."[18]

Of course, changing history is no simple matter. Even the Terminator was thwarted by defenders of the established chronicle of events. Recently, the Chinese government cracked down on historians who questioned the regime's accounts of the heroic actions of Chinese soldiers in a famous battle during the Second World War. The government accused these scholars of "Western-influenced skepticism," and "historical nihilism." A Beijing court found one historian guilty of libel for challenging the official history.[19]

Those seeking to revise history often battle against competing accounts and, even when they seemingly succeed in imposing a new narrative, they may struggle to eliminate artifacts that contain clues to the existence of some alternative interpretation of the past. In Philip K. Dick's dystopian novella *The Man in the High Castle*, the fascist rulers of an imaginary America that had been defeated by Nazi Germany search for years to find and destroy old newsreels that could raise doubts about the official version of history. In Soviet Russia, once-prominent figures who had fallen from favor were, usually without explanation, deleted from official news accounts and photographs as though they had never existed. This Soviet practice gave rise to the art of Kremlinology, which included scanning official records and photos to determine who was not there. Or, to return to our discussion of the Civil War and Reconstruction, in recent years artifacts such as statues, portraits, flags, and even the names of buildings that served as reminders of the old history of the Civil War and Reconstruction have been gradually removed and even erased because of their inconsistency with contemporary narratives.

This effort to erase the Confederate narrative has led to an uproar, not only over the monuments but over such things as a plan announced by HBO to air a television series set in an alternate America where the South had won the Civil War, seceded from the Union, and continued the institution of slavery into the present day. Many believe this alternate reality poses a threat to the present reality. "Nothing's settled, nothing's healed," one critic of HBO's plan observed.[20] Indeed, the past is never fully settled and remains open to conflicting narratives and periodic revision.

How the Future Affects the Present

Just as the past is affected by the present, the present can be affected by predictions or visions of the future. In the Hebrew Bible, Joseph's interpretation of Pharaoh's dream as a vision of the future brought the Hebrew leader great power in the present. In literature, moreover, time travelers often bring back knowledge from the future that can offer guidance to those living in the present. Thus, for example, in H. G. Wells's novel *The Time Machine*, the protagonist travels to the year A.D. 802,701. There he finds two quasi-human species, the Eloi and the Morlocks, both descended from different strata of contemporary humanity—the Eloi apparently from the bourgeoisie and the Morlocks from the proletariat. The Eloi live above ground and seem to do nothing but cavort in the sunshine while the Morlocks live deep below the surface where they tend ancient machines. The brutish Morlocks produce clothing for the playful Eloi but, at night, the Morlocks emerge from their caves to hunt and eat members of the other group. The point of the story is that, if allowed to continue, class conflict will produce a nightmarish world in which the industrial proletariat and contemporary bourgeoisie have been transformed into distinct species in a macabre relationship. Thus, by journeying into the distant future, the protagonist brings back an important lesson for the present.

The idea of the future affecting the present is not simply a fictional conceit. Indeed, the present is influenced by the future in several ways. The most obvious is expectations—current behavior is often guided by future expectations. As expectations of the future change, so does behavior in the present. This is a phenomenon well known to economists. Rational expectations theory in economics holds that individuals link their behavior in the marketplace to their expectations regarding future economic conditions. If individuals and corporations expect the government to stimulate the economy they will raise their prices or wage demands in anticipation of future inflation. The effect of such expectations may, themselves, be inflationary as if a possible future changed the present.[21]

Political scientists, particularly those who study voting, are also familiar with the importance of future expectations. Voters' choices at the polls are affected by their own, as well as expert, predictions about the electoral future. For instance, voters are well known to be reluctant to vote for third parties or primary candidates who seem to have no chance of winning. This is sometimes called the psychology of the lost vote, and, in response, candidates for political office work to convince potential supporters that they have a good chance of winning.[22] It is for this reason that preelection polls are so important. Voters, financial backers, and activists are likely to abandon candidates who are predicted to have little chance of success. In 2015, for example, the nominal front runner for the Republican presidential nomination, Governor Jeb Bush, saw his once-promising candidacy undermined by polls showing that his future prospects for victory against the Democrats were actually quite dim. Assessing these forecasts, some Bush supporters turned to other candidates, allowing the apparent future to alter their present-day behavior. Bush withdrew from the race in 2016 as his expectations worsened.

Expectations also play a role in assessing candidates' electoral performances. In primary contests, candidates' showings are often compared to preelection poll predictions. A candidate who garners more votes than expected is said to have done well while a candidate who underperforms the polls or other predictors often experiences an erosion of support as their future prospects seem to be less than had been expected. An interesting example of a politician actually driven from office as a result of future expectations is President Lyndon Johnson. In 1968, Johnson was the incumbent president and, despite the opposition of Democratic opponents of the Vietnam War, it was generally assumed that Johnson would easily secure the 1968 Democratic presidential nomination. So confident was Johnson that he did not bother to enter the March 1968 New Hampshire Democratic primary, which would be the first nominating contest to be held that year.

At the last minute, fearing the embarrassment of even a nominal victory by Johnson's opponent, Minnesota senator Eugene McCarthy, Johnson's supporters organized a write-in campaign. Such campaigns demand too much of voters and are usually futile. But, despite the fact that McCarthy's name was actually on the ballot and Johnson's was not, the result was a 7 percentage point victory for the president. Johnson's opponents in the national media, however, ignored the severe handicap faced by a write-in candidate and declared that Johnson had not performed as well as might have been expected of an incumbent. Johnson withdrew from the race, having in effect been defeated by future expectations invented by his political foes.

Competing political forces often seek to influence expectations by elaborating images of what they claim is a likely future if individuals in the present follow, or fail to follow, the prescriptions these forces offer. These future visions generally take the form of utopias or dystopias. A utopian future offers lessons about what to do in the present while a dystopian future offers lessons about what not to do. Some utopias and dystopias are religious in character, but many have been political. Karl Marx's writings, for example, offer a utopian vision of a future in which inequality has been abolished, a vision that influenced tens of millions of individuals to work toward its realization. Marx, of course, viewed himself as a scientific rather than utopian socialist, more concerned with how the working class was to destroy the old society than with the precise shape of the new one. Nevertheless, Marx credits utopian socialist writers such as Charles Fourier, Henri de Saint-Simon, and Robert Owen with developing a vision of a new world that enlightened the working class with possibilities and ideals toward which to work.[23] It was the utopian socialists, said Marx, who provided the revolutionary workers of the 1871 Paris Commune with their main goals—suppression of the wage system and the end of class rule.[24] The utopian future inspired political action in the present.

In the United States, Edward Bellamy's late nineteenth-century utopian novel, *Looking Backward*, was enormously popular, selling more than half a million copies.[25] The novel tells the story of a young man who falls asleep in the late nineteenth century and awakens in the year 2000 to find America transformed into a socialist paradise in which hunger and deprivation have been eliminated and all citizens enjoy a high standard of living. Bellamy's utopian novel sparked the formation of a political movement and the organization of more than one hundred political clubs seeking to alter the present to conform to Bellamy's depiction of the future.

The future also informs and affects the present through dystopian visions in which knowledge of the future serves as a warning of the dire consequences likely to occur if some present-day phenomenon is not confronted and changed. George Orwell's famous dystopian novel, *1984* (written in 1948), depicted a grim future in which totalitarianism had triumphed. After Donald Trump's victory in the 2016 American presidential election, liberals claimed to see in *1984* a warning of what Trump's victory could bring and used the novel as a call to arms for anti-Trump forces. To cite a European example, in 2015 well-known French novelist Michel Houellebecq created a sensation in Europe with the publication of *Soumission* (Submission).[26] Set in France in the near future, the novel describes events in France after an Islamic party comes to power. The new party seeks to impose Islamic law, compel all children to attend Muslim schools, ban women from the workplace, and otherwise transform France into a Muslim country. While the book was intended as a satire, it was seen as a clarion call by anti-immigration forces in Europe who pointed to the novel as a warning of the likely future if Muslim immigration was not brought to a halt.

Dystopian visions of the future have played a prominent role in American political history. Several important dystopian novels were penned, for example, during the Populist era and read as calls to action by hundreds of thousands of Americans. The general theme of these novels, usually set in the not-so-distant future, is that corrupt capitalists, in league with Jews and foreigners—a nod to the strong nativist element of Populism—have taken over the United States and reduced authentic Americans to subservience and penury. The most popular of these novels, though seldom read today, was Ignatius Donnelly's 1889 work, *Caesar's Column.*[27] Donnelly had served as the Populist lieutenant governor of Minnesota and was the author of the 1892 national Populist platform. He was also the editor of two leading Populist newspapers, the *Anti-Monopolist* and the *Representative. Caesar's Column*, which sold more than 250,000 copies, seeks to warn readers of the consequences of allowing contemporary political and economic tendencies to continue.

In the book, Donnelly's protagonist leaves a mythical Populist stronghold in Uganda to visit New York exactly 100 years in the future. He discovers that the leadership of the United States has fallen into the hands of a secretive group of greedy financiers. The leader of this group, Jacob Isaacs, calls himself "Prince Cabano." Ordinary Americans have become the unwitting slaves of the cabal. To its hundreds of thousands of readers, *Caesar's Column* seemed to illustrate real threats in the future that must be met by political action in the present. Its dystopian vision of the future helped to make Populism a powerful political force.

Competing forces, whether they represent governments, political parties, ideological and religious groups, economic interests, or other political combatants, often vie with one another to develop compelling utopian images of what the future will hold under their own dominion, frequently coupled with derogative views of a future controlled by their rivals. These images are designed to convince groups in the present to work toward a particular future and against the others. In effect, competing forces establish political bases in the future from which to guide present-day political action.

These images are typically abstract, but occasionally we see material depictions of rival visions of the political future. For example, during the 1930s some of the world's major competing political regimes spent millions constructing elaborate futuristic world's fairs to concretely exhibit their own visions of the future and demonstrate their manifest technical and ideological superiority to their national rivals.[28] The *New York Times's* foreign correspondent, Anne O'Hare McCormick, called these fairs "national projections" on the part of liberal, communist, and fascist powers, each seeking to promote its own claims to the future.[29] Thus, for example, the 1937 Dusseldorf fair was designed to highlight the achievements of National Socialism and to illustrate a future in which industrial production, technology, and art, all revitalized by Nazism, would produce a strong, prosperous, and united Germany. For its part, America's 1939 World's Fair, calling itself the "Fair of the Future," was explicitly designed to illustrate "the building of a new and better future." This future, in which ordinary Americans would benefit from amazing new industrial products and scientific discoveries, was to be produced by the giants of American industry working for the public good. The fair emphasized that for American industry, as General Electric's advertising slogan later put it, "progress is our most important product."[30]

By presenting competing visions of the future, national and ideological competitors sought to rally support for themselves in the present. The future became another battleground to help determine the contemporary balance of power. Lest anyone think that these competing views of the future had no effect upon the present, it behooves us to remember that for nearly a decade millions sacrificed their lives on behalf of competing communist, fascist, and liberal visions of the future world.

How the Future Affects the Past

Not only does the future have an impact upon the present, it can affect the past as well. Often, individuals or groups with a particular vision of the future will seek to identify elements in the past that seem to portend or validate their predictions for the future. If necessary they will reinterpret the past to achieve consistency with their imagined future. One example of this phenomenon is Friedrich Engels's well-known nineteenth-century work, The *Origin of the Family, Private Property and the State*.[31] In this work, Engels presents an interpretation of anthropological findings, particularly the work of Lewis Henry Morgan, to identify in primitive society a number of features that Engels, along with Marx, viewed as desirable goals for the future. Engels averred that Morgan's anthropological data showed that primitive societies were essentially collective, not divided into classes of exploiters and exploited, and that lands were held in common and tools and utensils were owned directly by those who used them.[32]

While nominally basing his work on Morgan's findings, Engels frequently revised Morgan's analyses to conform more closely to Marxist thought. One point made by Morgan with which Engels fully agreed and which he used to close his own book is Morgan's view of the future as "a revival, in a higher form, of the liberty, equality and fraternity of the ancient gentes." Thus, Engels's excursion into the past was guided by his vision of the future. In effect, the future created the past. In a similar vein, Benito Mussolini told Italians that his vision of a powerful and prosperous Italy was confirmed by the glory of the Roman Empire. Mussolini claimed to have searched Roman history and to have found in it many facts and themes that, if properly understood, presaged Italy's future greatness.[33]

More recently, the leaders of ISIS worked to inspire their followers by imagining an Islamic history consistent with their future vision of a powerful new Islamic caliphate. Jihadists, according to one scholar, are particularly "infatuated" with the great eighth-century Abbasid caliph Harun al-Rashid whose caliphate they view as the golden age of Islam and a model for the future. However, to make this history consistent with their present-day views, jihadists have been compelled to substantially rewrite it, particularly excising Harun's heterodox religious views, unorthodox sexual preferences, and his apparent love of wine. Since this established history is inconsistent with the fundamentalist interpretations of Islam favored by the leaders of ISIS, history has been revised to fit contemporary preferences and visions of the future.[34]

On Time

By viewing past, present, and future as interactive, we have adopted what is known as an "eternalist" view of time. It is worth pausing to consider what this view entails. The three main philosophical conceptions of time are eternalism, presentism, and, albeit with fewer adherents than the two other perspectives, the growing universe view. From the eternalist perspective, past, present, and future exist simultaneously and possess equivalent ontological status. In the presentist view, only the present exists.[35] From the growing universe perspective, the past and present exist while the future does not. The passage of time, which occurs in the present, continually adds more to the past—hence the growing universe.

Of these three perspectives, presentism seems most consistent with commonsense observation. The present is real, the past is in retreat, and the future uncertain. One difficulty with presentism, though, is that there are objects and events about which we speak and of whose past or probable future existence we are aware that do not exist in the present. Often, we can even make meaningful comparisons among past objects and we are aware of the impact they had on the present. For example, Franklin Roosevelt served four terms in office and brought about the enactment of many laws that continue to affect the United States. James Buchanan, on the other hand, was elected only once and accomplished little. Neither individual exists in the present but their past existence is recalled in the present and, despite the fact that neither exists, meaningful statements can be made describing and comparing the two. By the same token, the future has not yet arrived but as we sit preparing for a predicted snowfall, the future is exerting considerable influence over our actions in the present. Most versions of presentism, moreover, seem to contradict the special theory of relativity by assuming the existence of a unique present.[36]

The growing universe theory does not suffer from the first problem of presentism; it acknowledges the reality of past objects and events. However, by denying the reality of the future, it ignores the fact that in the present we have probabilistic knowledge of the future, such as the weather forecast, and ideas about the future that can affect behavior in the present. As we noted above, rational expectations have become fundamental to macroeconomic models, to take but one example.

Our perspective in this book is eternalist in that we view past, present, and future as existing simultaneously and interacting with one another. Some neuroscientists argue that humans are in effect psychological eternalists showing concurrent awareness of past, present, and future. Endel Tulving dubbed this phenomenon "chronesthesia."[37] Allen Bluedorn has conducted a number of interesting experiments that seem to confirm cognitive connections between the past and future.[38] Our perspective, though, would have to be seen as one of quasi-eternalism. Influenced by the ideas of Peter Forrest, we assign special ontological status to the present because the past and future lack their own sentience, deriving sentience, instead, from the present.[39] This quasi-eternalist perspective actually has elements in common with ontological presentism though we assign the present a special ontological status without denying the reality fof the past and future. From our perspective, the past was real; though presently lacking sentience, the past is susceptible to animation and revision from the present. The ontological status of the future is somewhat more problematic. Viewed from the present, the future is more indefinite than the past and similarly lacking in sentience. Events that have not yet occurred may never take place, but the future can be animated from the present as it is described predictively and probabilistically. Once animated, the future can affect the present, and perhaps even the past.

Note that our concept of eternalism does not accept logical fatalism, or the idea that past, present, and future are givens, with which eternalism is sometimes conflated. Quite the contrary. Immutability is not a necessary condition for the reality of the future. From our perspective, past, present, and future are all real but indeterminate—in play, so to speak, and influenced by one another.

In the remaining pages of this book we shall present a narrative discussion and a series of experiments designed to measure the impact of past, present, and future upon one another—at least in the political realm. Chapter 2 will examine the relationship between the past and the present. Chapter 3 will address the relationship between the future and the present. Chapter 4 will examine the ties between the future and the past. Chapter 5 will offer a number of reflections on the political uses of time. In our discussion and experiments we shall see that the interrelationships we are examining have enormous potential as political tools. In science fiction films, people travel into their past and future in order to enhance their power in their own present. Those able to make use of political time travel may also increase their political power in the present. Indeed, those who control the past and future are likely to control the present as well.

CHAPTER 2

Reshaping the Past to Change the Present

As we saw in chapter 1, when governments or important political forces seek to bring about major changes in current political and social realities, they often find it useful to rewrite accepted history to conform with and bolster the new truths they espouse. "In extinguishing a kingdom of men," said nineteenth-century Chinese poet Gong Zizhen, "the first step is to remove its history." Quantum theory might say those revising history were emphasizing one over another of the infinite number of paths that might have led to the same point. Through such changes of emphasis, older understandings of past events may be altered, debunked, or dismissed to make the historical record more consistent with contemporary preferences. As political scientist Linda B. Miller has observed, present-day policymakers will search in the "grab-bag of history" for facts, analogies, and orientations, choosing those they deem useful while ignoring those inconsistent with their current goals.[1]

In some instances, facts and even individuals are allowed to fade from history as though they never existed and are, perhaps, replaced with new facts more consistent with currently favored perspectives. Such reinvention of the narrative of the past can be useful for a number of reasons. Reimagined pasts might highlight injustices that require redress or ancient glories that should be restored. Perhaps the record requires correction to convert saints into sinners and sinners into saints or, on a larger scale, former allies into foes and former foes into friends. Perhaps the past contains politically potent symbols of old loyalties that new ruling groups would prefer to expunge from the collective consciousness. Perhaps national honor can be salvaged by a tight focus on French or Dutch resistance to the Nazi occupation when the true norm was passivity and collaboration.

Understandings of the past can have important behavioral consequences for the present. Reminding governments of an obligation made in the past may force them into unwanted courses of action in the present lest they lose their credibility. Grievances and hatreds accumulated in the past, as we shall see in chapter 4, can lead to violent and even barbaric behavior in the present. Political ties forged in the past affect voting and other forms of political conduct in the present. And, while it may be true that politics is driven by interests, these interests are, themselves, often products of ideologies that may, in turn, be shaped by some understanding of history. China, for example, views itself as having sovereignty over Taiwan. This interest may be defined more by history than by economic or strategic concerns, though all coincide in this case. If national interests were determined purely by material interest, might England not be better off without Scotland? Yet, mainly on the basis of shared history, most in England hoped that the Scottish independence referendum of 2014 would fail. And contemporary German foreign and immigration policy would be difficult to understand without reference to Germany's past.[2]

What people think about the past, including commitments, grievances, loyalties, and so forth, is certainly subject to reimagination and revision, with implications for the present. As we observed in chapter 1, an ideational change regarding the past may subsequently materialize in the present as some perspectives seem to be confirmed and others refuted by a reinvented past. Yet, once agreed upon, history is not so easily rewritten. The past is malleable, but its malleability is that of pig iron, not putty. Long-accepted versions of the past often have defenders who resist efforts to rewrite a history that is consistent with their own present-day preferences. In the years following World War II, writes historian Konrad Jarausch, increasing numbers of German academics, journalists, and politicians promoted a critical view of the German past while millions of ordinary Germans clung to a more positive recollection of the Third Reich, leading to debates over which version of the past should be recognized by monuments, museums, and public celebrations.[3]

Struggles among groups favoring alternative historical concepts often do not produce fully conclusive outcomes. Forces that have won control over the present may spend decades seeking to erase artifacts that serve as reminders of a past they hope to see forgotten. For example, after their conquest of the Inca Empire in the sixteenth century, the realm's new Spanish overlords sought to erase all vestiges of Inca history, language, religion, and culture to diminish resistance to their rule. Such resistance, however, continued for decades, led by members of the Inca nobility or *panaqa*. The *panaqa* fought to maintain the memory of the Inca Empire, among other things seeking to protect their empire's most important religious symbols, particularly the mummified remains of former emperors, widely venerated as sacred objects. Members of the *panaqa* endured death by torture at the hands of the Spaniards to prevent these sacred mummies from falling into Spanish hands.[4] The Spaniards, for their part, viewed the mummies and the history they symbolized as a threat to their own power and hunted for them for nearly three decades before finding and destroying the last of them.

Champions of once prevalent but now generally disbelieved historical narratives can be found throughout the world. In modern-day Japan, quite a number of conservative politicians and historians dispute the conventional history of World War II, asserting that Japan's actions were based upon a principle of self-defense against Western imperialism. In Germany and elsewhere, groups of "Holocaust deniers" object to the official history of Nazi atrocities and assert that these accounts are overblown if not complete fabrications. In the years immediately after World War II, the German Federal Republic and its American patron were sufficiently concerned that Germans might still accept this narrative that Holocaust denial was made a crime under the German Constitution.

It is important to note also that battles over linguistic policy are usually contests about alternative histories. In the eighteenth and nineteenth centuries, for example, the French central government successfully campaigned to stamp out such indigenous provincial languages as Normand and Breton that served as portals to a historical narrative not dominated by the rulers of Paris.[5] As these rulers knew, the survival of an old tongue can facilitate the recollection of an old history.

Revising History

George Orwell dramatized the idea of historical revisionism in his novel *1984*. The protagonist, Winston Smith, works as a minor functionary at the "Ministry of Truth." Smith's job entails revising old newspaper articles to make certain that leaders' predictions and pronouncements always turn out to be accurate. Smith is also assigned the task of erasing historical facts inconsistent with current policies. These inconvenient former facts are excised from the historical record by being dropped into the "memory hole," an opening leading to the ministry's enormous incinerator.

Orwell intended his novel to be a parody of efforts by various British social service agencies to rewrite history. The practices it describes, however, seem closer to those employed in Stalin's USSR where party leaders who incurred Stalin's displeasure were not only killed but also erased from the documentary record. Official news stories and photos were revised to delete all mention of these unfortunate individuals. Officially, they had never existed. For example, Nikolai Yezhov, head of the Soviet secret police, fell out of favor with Stalin in 1938 and was tortured and executed in 1940. Subsequently, Yezhov's name was removed from records and documents and his image excised from all official photos. Yezhov had become an "unperson," and has only been posthumously resurrected in recent years.[6] These sorts of official erasures have a long history. In ancient Rome, disgraced officials could be punished by a decree of *damnation memoriae* or condemnation of memory, which entailed removing every trace of the individual's existence, including official records, pictures, and statues. The individual thus condemned had officially never existed and might eventually fade from memory.

North Korea has taken official revision of history to a new extreme. In 2013, after paramount leader Kim Jong-un executed his uncle and former vice premier, Jang Song Thaek, Mr. Jang's name and photo were expunged from all official accounts and documents. It seemed that he had never existed. Subsequently, North Korea proceeded to erase 99 percent of its official news archive. Only articles published since the ascension of Kim Jong-un, and a small number of laudatory articles published about Kim before he took power, were retained. As a result, North Korea's official history now appears to begin with the current Mr. Kim.[7]

How to Reinvent the Past

Efforts to revise history can make use of a variety of instruments. Among the most common and powerful are television and film. As one commentator observed, "Movies are the source of much of what we know—or think we know—about history."[8] Historical films, however, do more than reenact the past. Instead, they reimagine the past to comport with some particular set of values or goals in the present. The importance of the historical film, avers film professor Robert Burgoyne, is that, "by reenacting the past in the present, the historical film brings the past into dialogue with the present."[9]

Such a dialogue can become especially evident during a period of crisis in the present when historical films can offer counsel and guidance derived from a reinvented past. In World War II England, for example, with a German invasion seemingly imminent, the government turned to film, in particular to historical narrative, to bolster popular unity and remind citizens that many times, in centuries past, the people of the British Isles had stood together against invaders and won despite the odds against them. Such a narrative is exemplified by the 1940 film *This England*, which was filmed during the Blitz and depicted a largely invented history of British steadfastness through the centuries that was designed to set an example of proper behavior in the face of calamity and adversity.[10]

During the same period, the Soviet Union turned to Russian history to rally its own citizens against the Germans. One of the great Soviet films of the late 1930s and early 1940s is Sergei Eisenstein's epic, *Alexander Nevsky*. The film tells the story of a thirteenth-century Russian prince who is shown rallying the common people of Novgorod to defeat the Teutonic knights who have invaded the land. To help viewers catch the connection between the knights and contemporary Germans, the helmets worn by the thirteenth-century invaders are emblazoned with swastikas.[11]

In interviews, the director compared Prince Alexander to Joseph Stalin, Russia's contemporary savior. *Nevsky* was released in 1938 and heavily promoted by the Soviet government though some critics questioned its historical accuracy. In 1939, after the USSR signed a nonaggression treaty with Nazi Germany, *Nevsky* was abruptly withdrawn from circulation, its historical account no longer consistent with contemporary political realities. Apparently, however, the government was prescient enough to realize that the history depicted by the film, though presently false, might someday again become true. Accordingly, copies of the film were only put into storage rather than destroyed. After June 1941, when the Germans invaded the Soviet Union, *Nevsky* quickly reappeared in cinemas throughout the USSR. In this rather peculiar way, history proved the old adage and repeated itself.

In the United States, during the economic struggles and hardships of the 1930s, the Hollywood Production Code Administration, an organization that today might be called a quasi-public entity, was created by the major film studios in collaboration with the government to monitor the content of motion pictures. Among its other projects, the Production Code Administration worked with Metro-Goldwyn-Mayer (MGM) studios to rewrite American history, producing a semidocumentary film combining footage from newsreels and old movies to offer a panoramic interpretation of U.S. history from colonial times to the present. This interpretation was filled with optimism about America designed to combat the pessimism produced by the Great Depression. The film's overall theme was outlined by its screenwriter, Jeannie Macpherson: "The theme we are trying to bring out in this story of America is LIBERTY (governmental and individual); EQUALITY (all races, all creeds) FREEDOM (speech, personal, press) PURSUIT OF HAPPINESS (for all men). The film presents American history as a 'massive and magnificent struggle for greatness.'"[12] To focus on the struggle for greatness meant omitting the more unsavory elements of American history, such as slavery, extermination of Native Americans, racism, ethnic hatreds, and economic exploitation. History was substantially revised to comport with the particular political needs of the present.

Historical revisionism in the movies became very pronounced before and during World War II as the government shifted from an isolationist stance to one of opposition to Nazi Germany and support for Britain and Russia and worked to create a supportive climate of public opinion for this transformation. During the early and mid-1930s, filmmakers and broadcasters had been reluctant to take a strong position on Germany in part for fear of offending pro-German and isolationist groups in the U.S. Joseph Breen, head of the Production Code Administration, often warned Hollywood against making anti-Nazi and "Communistic" propaganda films.[13]

Breen's predecessor, Will Hays, had held a similar view and had blocked production of several films deemed offensive to Nazi Germany such as an adaptation of Sinclair Lewis's *It Can't Happen Here*, as well as the antiwar film *Idiot's Delight*, which criticized Mussolini's invasion of Ethiopia. The film was eventually shown but only after scenes to which the Italian government objected were cut.[14]

By the late 1930s, the Roosevelt administration, having determined to shift away from isolationism and adopt a more confrontational posture toward the Germans, was pressing Hollywood to present the rise of Nazism and the actions of the Germans during the past several years in a more negative light. The result was a spate of films critical of Germany. One memorable film was Warner Brothers's 1938 film, *Confessions of a Nazi Spy*, starring Edward G. Robinson. The film was inspired by the actual case of a group of German spies who had come to the United States and were subsequently caught and convicted of espionage. When the film project was first being discussed, the German consul in Los Angeles wrote to the Production Code Administration urging that the project not be undertaken lest it lead to unspecified "difficulties."[15] Warner Brothers went ahead with the film and, indeed, put it in the hands of a staunchly anti-Nazi production crew. *Confessions* was directed by Anatol Litvak, a German-Jewish émigré, and starred Edward G. Robinson, a Jewish actor active in the Hollywood anti-Nazi movement, and Paul Lucas, another German-Jewish émigré. In the film, Nazi Germany is depicted as intent on world domination and as presenting a clear and present danger to the United States. Robinson, in the role of an FBI agent, asserts that through espionage and subversion Germany has already embarked on a war against the United States. Toward the conclusion of the film the audience is warned that continued isolationism could leave the United States and its way of life vulnerable to German attack from within and without.

By 1940, Hollywood studios were producing many feature films and film shorts promoting American rearmament and attacking Germany. Warner Brothers offered to make any film short on the need for military preparedness free of charge. At the Roosevelt administration's request, MGM produced a film on foreign and defense policy entitled *Eyes of the Navy*, which dramatically presented the importance of a strong national defense and an activist foreign policy. Other studios followed with films bearing such titles as *I Wanted Wings*, *Dive Bomber*, *Flight Command*, *Navy Blues*, *Buck Private*, and *Tanks a Million*. Even the comedy team of Abbott and Costello promoted preparedness with their humorous depiction of national military service, *Caught in the Draft*. Other important films presenting anti-German themes or warning of the need for preparedness included *A Yank in the R.A.F.*, in which after piloting a British fighter for several years, a young American flier shows his countrymen how to fight the Nazis, and Warner Brothers' *Sergeant York*, the story of America's greatest World War I hero, Alvin York, who put aside his pacifism to serve his country in the previous war against Germany. York, himself, attended the film's New York premiere along with Eleanor Roosevelt and General John

Pershing. York declared that if Americans stopped fighting for freedom, "then we owe the memory of George Washington an apology."[16]

As Hollywood began to present a negative account of German history, the history of the Soviet Union received a substantial cinematic facelift. Before World War II, most Americans hated and feared the Soviet Union and its dictator, Joseph Stalin, and for good reason. Stalinist Russia was one of the most brutal and repressive regimes on the face of the earth. When Nazi Germany invaded the USSR in 1941, Americans saw the two dictatorships as morally equivalent and could see little reason to favor one over the other. Some, indeed, thought Nazism was preferable to "godless" Communism. This was a view particularly promoted among American Catholics by the Vatican, which had reached an accommodation with Hitler but feared the anticlerical agenda associated with Bolshevism.

The U.S. government, though, believed that Germany posed an existential threat to the United States and to its foremost ally, England, and hoped to prevent a German victory. Accordingly, the Roosevelt administration sought to shift public attitudes toward Russia to allow, first, material support in the form of lend-lease aid, and eventually military coordination in the war against Germany. The government turned to the Hollywood film studios, which were already being asked to produce anti-Nazi films, and asked them to produce movies presenting the Soviet Union in a more favorable light, in effect rewriting the past quarter century of Russian history. Hollywood filmmakers had their own reasons to support the government and turned to their task with some enthusiasm, producing a number of films promoting a positive view of recent Russian history.

Among the best known of these films was *Song of Russia*, an MGM production starring Robert Taylor who plays an American conductor on a musical tour of the Soviet Union just before the German invasion. Taylor falls in love with a beautiful Russian pianist and the two visit many idyllic Russian cities before their lives are disrupted by the Germans. The film depicts Stalin's Russia as a peaceful and happy place, populated by generally contented citizens not so different from ordinary Americans—hence the love affair between the American and the Russian. The brutality of the Soviet regime is nowhere in evidence and the Russians encountered are proud of having rebuilt their country from the wreckage of the tsarist empire. The film was a commercial success and was viewed by several million Americans.

An even more important film designed to rewrite Russian history was

Warner Brothers' 1943 film *Mission to Moscow*. The movie was based on the 1941 book by former U.S. ambassador to the Soviet Union Joseph E. Davies and was produced in response to a request by President Franklin D. Roosevelt who wished to bolster public support for America's alliance with Russia. In the book and the film, Ambassador Davies, portrayed in the movie by Walter Huston, arrives in Moscow with his family in 1936. Davies is initially deeply suspicious of the Soviet regime but slowly learns that Stalin is a trustworthy ally and that Soviet citizens are well treated by their government and live comfortably. Stalin's infamous show trials, in which a large number of high-ranking officials and military officers were sentenced to death on the basis of confessions extracted under torture, are depicted as proper judicial hearings aimed at punishing self-confessed German spies and other criminals. In the film, Ambassador Davies declares, "No leaders of a nation have been so misrepresented and misunderstood as those in the Soviet government." The U.S. Office of War Information reviewed the film before its release and declared that it would help Americans to understand their Russian allies and to see that Russian leaders were well-intentioned statesmen, not the murderous thugs Americans had previously thought them to be.[17]

This officially sponsored revision of Soviet history was successful and opened the way for lend-lease aid to the Russians, something that had previously been opposed by public opinion and congressional majorities. Revision of the past had changed the present—and the future.

With the end of World War II and the advent of the Cold War, American filmmakers were prodded by Congress and various government agencies to again rewrite the Soviet history they had so recently invented. Between the 1940s and the 1970s, the once friendly Russians were reimagined as ruthless, dangerous, and perhaps even more murderous than the defeated Germans. Hundreds of films focused on Soviet espionage in the United States as well as the Soviet Union's plans for world conquest. Such titles as *I Married a Communist, The Red Menace, I Was a Communist for the FBI*, along with the U.S. government documentary *Communist Blueprint for Conquest*, illustrate the point.

In motion pictures produced during the war, Americans often married Russians, symbolically joining forces against the Germans. Now, in films like *The Big Lift*, dramatizing the 1948–49 Berlin airlift, American fliers fell in love with and married German women, forming a marital alliance against the Russians to symbolize the actual alliance then taking form.

To underscore this new present, the Russian past was also cinematically reinvented. In place of *Mission to Moscow*'s uplifting account of Soviet history, *Dr Zhivago* offered a portrait of hardship and terror in the creation of the Soviet state while *One Day in the Life of Ivan Denisovich* presented a harrowing account of the daily lives of the prisoners in Soviet labor camps. *Guilty of Treason* depicted Soviet suppression of religion by examining the treatment of Hungary's Roman Catholic prelate, Joseph Cardinal Mindszenty. The Cardinal is beaten, tortured, and imprisoned after Hungary becomes a Soviet satellite state in 1948. Mindszenty, nevertheless, refuses to renounce his faith and succumb to the godless Russians.

In some instances, this historical revision took the form of reediting existing films. One example of this form of revisionism is *The North Star* (later retitled as *Armored Attack*), a 1943 film about the resistance of Ukrainian villagers, through guerrilla tactics, against the German invaders of the Ukrainian SSR. The film presents an idealized portrait of life on a Soviet collective farm before the war and a sympathetic account of Soviet citizens and their devotion to their nation. In the 1950s, the House Un-American Activities Committee cited *North Star* as an example of pro-Soviet propaganda. The producers responded with cuts, edits, and new footage. In the new version, life on Soviet collective farms is seen as filled with toil, hardship, and privation. The hapless villagers are now brutalized by both Russian and German soldiers with the former receiving more censure than the latter. It would hardly be unfair to call the recutting of the film "Orwellian."[18]

A recent example of the power of film to rewrite historical memory is the 2020 Spanish documentary, *The Silence of Others*. The film presents the ongoing effort to make public the government's crimes during the Franco era when tens of thousands of Spaniards were imprisoned, tortured, and murdered by the regime. After Franco's death in 1975, the nation's major political parties agreed upon what was called the "Pact of Forgetting," a decision to avoid any discussion of Francoism or to make any effort to identify or punish the perpetrators of the heinous crimes committed by the regime. Politicians deemed "forgetting" to be necessary to bury unpleasant questions about the past and to facilitate national reconciliation. The pact was formalized in Spain's 1977 Amnesty Law. The law blocked efforts by citizens even to determine the fate of babies stolen at birth and awarded to loyalist families, or to learn the fates of relatives and loved ones who disappeared in the regime's prisons. Generally speaking, "forgetting" was a success and younger Spaniards know little about the Franco era.

After its release, *The Silence of Others* caused a sensation in Spain where, within months, it had been viewed by more than a million individuals. The film reviews the crimes of the Franco government, reveals the names of perpetrators, and depicts the ways in which decades of Spain's past had been erased. The film restores a past that had been all but forgotten. By revealing the crimes of respected elders, the duplicity of the nation's entire political class, and even causing individuals to question their parentage, the film has upended Spanish society and altered the contours of the nation's political alliances. By revising the collective remembrance of the past, *The Silence of Others* has shaken the foundations of the present.

Textbooks

Another important instrument of historical revisionism is the prosaic secondary school textbook. Secondary school texts both reflect and reinforce particular historical understandings and potentially influence the ways in which history will be understood by the next generation of citizens. Hence, these texts often become the focal points for controversies among groups and forces with divergent historical understandings that are usually tied to differing political and social agendas in the present. For example, in the 1920s, Mayor William "Big Bill" Thompson of Chicago, seeking the favor of the city's many Irish voters, condemned the history texts then being used in Chicago's schools as manifesting a pro-British slant. Thompson demanded that new texts be developed that eliminated this alleged bias and, instead, properly recognize the achievements of Irish Americans.

Thomson's demands set off a brawl among the city's ethnic groups, with each demanding that history texts feature their own contribution to the nation's glorious past. Italians and Norwegians argued over whether credit for the discovery of America should be given to Christopher Columbus or Leif Erikson. Poles complained about a history text that identified Revolutionary War hero Casimir Pulaski as a Lithuanian while Lithuanians objected to a book that declared Thaddeus Kosciuszko to have been a Pole. Both men, it seems, were of mixed heritage. African Americans advocated for the inclusion of a number of Black luminaries in history texts while Native Americans sought coverage for Pocahontas, Tecumseh, and Chief Joseph. The Ku Klux Klan objected to the inclusion of Blacks and Native Americans and also demanded the removal from the texts of a number of Roman Catholics whom the Klan thought unworthy of inclusion in America's historical record.[19]

Today, a growing matter of contestation is the textbook treatment of the history of Islam. In a seventh-grade world history text currently used in a number of school districts in the U.S., a section entitled "Muslim Empires" explains that Islam spread peacefully and that its success was facilitated by the tolerance shown by Muslims toward Jews and Christians. This historical account is contested by groups pointing out that the spread of Islam included conquest and forced conversion and that its record of religious tolerance was at best mixed.[20] This dispute over Islamic history is obviously driven by competing interpretations of the role of Islam in the modern world.

Historian Joseph Moreau has identified several major periods of conflict in the United States over the content of history texts.[21] In the immediate aftermath of the Civil War, secondary school texts, then mainly published in New England, promoted the idea that Southern secession had been illicit and that slavery had been morally wrong. Former Confederate vice president Alexander Stephens responded by writing a neo-Confederate textbook that presented the war as a battle between the states over the terms of national union and defended the emergent Jim Crow system as necessary for the welfare of both Black and White southerners. For a time, various veterans' groups, state governments, and interest groups dueled over these competing historical interpretations and many publishers promoted different books in the northern and southern markets. By the later decades of the nineteenth century, though, the neo-Confederate history fit well with the growing racism and nativism of the North and, as we saw in chapter 1, most Americans accepted the thesis of southern victimization. Textbook publishers found that they no longer were compelled to publish distinct northern and southern texts. The neo-Confederate vision of history had triumphed, at least for a time.

Other textbook controversies concerned matters of ethnicity, social class, and race. In the 1920s, as we saw above, advocates for various immigrant groups asserted that history texts focused on the achievements of White Anglo-Saxon Protestants, ignoring the contributions of other groups to American society and culture. They demanded that history texts move away from "Anglo-Saxonism" to a more inclusive narrative. Parallel demands were echoed time and again as spokespersons for unionized workers, African Americans, women, Asians, and Latinos demanded that history texts be revised to give due recognition to the achievements of the members of their group. Each of these demands was, in turn, resisted by defenders of the established historical narrative who saw demands for change as efforts to falsify the historical narrative for contemporary political purposes. Often, such battles were fought and refought as losing forces refused to surrender their historical claims.

In 2015, Texas was embroiled in a fight over the appropriate treatment of the Civil War in secondary school history texts. Some members of the state board of education wished to assign texts that presented states' rights as the chief issue of the Civil War while other board members wanted to choose texts that focused on slavery. Like most of the nation, by the 1990s Texas had accepted the centrality of slavery in its history texts. In 2010, however, a group of conservative board members was able to take control of the texts and order history to be rewritten. The current controversy stems from an effort by another group of board members to revise history again, this time to restore the narrative to its pre-2010 version.[22]

Present and Past: Patterns of Change

As these examples suggest, contending forces in the present believe they have a stake in the ways in which secondary school texts treat the past. Though ongoing, this concern seems most pronounced when some new set of political forces achieves prominence and, in particular, control of state and local school boards in the present, and works to consolidate its power by reaching into and reimagining the past. The historic pattern of textbook revision in the United States is consistent with these shifts in political power. History, it seems, can be revised by those who win control over the printing presses.

The Malleable Past

The United States is hardly the only country in which victorious political forces rewrite school textbooks and engage in other efforts to force history to conform to new political understandings. Indeed, several nations have rewritten their own histories two or three times in the past century as war and political upheaval produced major transformations in their government and politics. Take the case of Germany. In the 1930s, with the ascension of Adolph Hitler and the Nazis, German history was substantially revised to report past events from a Nazi perspective.

To begin with, the Nazis sought to revise the history of Germany's defeat in World War I. According to accounts accepted by Germany's left-liberal regime, and taught in the schools, the war had been mainly the fault of Prussian militarists who had been more than willing to shed the blood of ordinary Germans in the pursuit of their own imperial ambitions. Having launched an unwinnable war against much of the world, Germany faced an inevitable defeat that exposed the corruption of the Prussian monarchy and the cupidity and avarice of the small cadre of industrialists who hoped to benefit from the war. In this historical narrative, the liberal Weimar regime was the best hope for solving Germany's deep-seated social and economic problems and making Germany part of a peaceful Europe.

The Nazis completely rejected this historical narrative and, indeed, removed from library shelves and burned thousands of books that exemplified elements of this now-illicit history. New textbooks presented a revised history in which German soldiers had fought heroically for the Fatherland only to be "stabbed in the back" (the *Dolchstoss* theory) by a conspiracy of Communists, Jews, and other traitors.[23] In the resulting Versailles Treaty of 1919, signed by turncoat members of the German government, the vengeful victors stripped Germany of a great deal of its territory and agricultural and industrial potential. With the rise to power of Hitler and the Nazi Party, however, Germany began to resume its rightful place in the world. Hitler restored German military power, recovered Germany's lost territories and possessions, and sought vengeance for the treason and national humiliation of 1919. According to the new texts, the Second World War was triggered by the aggressive actions of the British and French and by the Poles' abuse of ethnic Germans living in Poland.

During the Nazi era, elementary and secondary school texts also emphasized anti-Semitism. Teachers were required to spend a good deal of classroom time discussing Nazi racial theory and "the Jewish problem." Jews were portrayed as enemies of the German people, cunning swindlers, sexual perverts, and so forth. The Nazi's anti-Semitic educational campaign required a revision of the textbook account of the place of Jews in German history. Jews had, of course, lived in Germany for centuries and made substantial contributions to German science, German industry, and

German culture. Indeed, Jews had been instrumental in the unification of modern Germany and the construction of the German state.[24]

This conventional narrative was replaced by a very different account. The manual issued to German teachers in 1937 declared, "The National Socialist state requires its teachers to teach German children racial theory. For the German people, racial theory means the Jewish problem."[25] The manual presents a version of world history that implicates Jews in the destruction of a number of major civilizations such as Egypt, Persia, and Rome. In each instance, the Jews burrowed from within to undermine the culture and economy of the host nation. Teachers were urged to draw parallels with Germany where the Jews were also "infiltrators" who sought to sap the nation's economic and political power and to destroy the German people. Teachers are told to explain that Jewish efforts to infiltrate German society, as they had been able to do elsewhere, led the government to issue the Nuremberg laws, mandating strict social separation between Jews and Aryans and extruding Jews from German's government, educational system, and commerce.

German cinema in the Nazi years also became an important propaganda tool and, indeed, Nazi propaganda minister Joseph Goebbels proclaimed himself "patron of the German film." More than one thousand films were produced by German movie studios between 1933 and 1945. Many focused on the heroes of the German past such as Frederick the Great and Otto von Bismarck and sought to wrap the current regime in their mantle. For example, in a 1942 film biography of Bismarck, entitled *Die Entlassung* (The Dismissal), as he leaves office, Bismarck says, "My work is done. It was only a beginning. Who will complete it?"[26] Presumably the audience should have no difficulty answering the question.

Jews were a major target of cinematic revisionism. Nazi cinema acknowledged the fact that Jews had been prominent in German history. Films, however, focused on some of these prominent Jews to show that they had actually been villainous and destructive. The most famous anti-Semitic film of the Nazi era is the 1940 film *Jud Suss*, nominally a biography of the Jewish financier Joseph Suss Oppenheimer, banker and financial adviser to Duke Karl Alexander of Wurttemberg during the duke's five-year reign from 1732 to 1737. Oppenheimer was one of the "court Jews" who managed the fiscal affairs of many German principalities during this period.[27] Lacking financial acumen and access to international financial markets, even such exalted German noble families as the Habsburgs and Hohenzollerns relied on their court Jews to finance their wars and extravagant lifestyles. One court Jew, Gershon von Bleichroeder, in the service of Otto von Bismarck, created the financial foundations for the unification of the German Reich. Acting in the names of their noble patrons, these court Jews could be very powerful but inevitably made important enemies. Usually their influence and sometimes their lives ended with their patron's death or downfall.

The aforementioned Karl Alexander was an experienced soldier and somewhat ruthless individual who had governed the Kingdom of Serbia with an iron hand under the authority of the Holy Roman emperor. When he inherited the Duchy of Wurttemberg in 1732, Karl Alexander moved his court to Stuttgart. He put Oppenheimer in charge of the duchy's finances and set about squeezing as much revenue as he could from his new subjects. When Karl Alexander died unexpectedly in 1737, Oppenheimer was arrested by the late duke's many political enemies. Charged with a variety of financial and moral crimes, Oppenheimer was executed in 1738.

The Oppenheimer case was a somewhat obscure and not extraordinary episode in German court history, though Oppenheimer had been the subject of a sympathetic fictional portrayal in 1925. For Nazi filmmakers Oppenheimer's downfall became an opportunity to ascribe a mendacious and licentious nature to Jewish people. Oppenheimer is presented as having corrupted the honest, albeit naive young duke and so enmeshed him in financial frauds that the duke saw no escape. Consistent with the theme of Jewish infiltration, Oppenheimer is shown usurping the duke's authority and behaving as though he, and not Karl Alexander, was the duchy's ruler. To make matters even worse, Oppenheimer forces himself upon virtuous German women. The film's heroine kills herself after being forced to have sex with the financier. In the end, the citizens of Wurttemberg revolt and capture and hang Oppenheimer—a just punishment for his crimes. Production of *Jud Suss* was overseen personally by Joseph Goebbels, and judged by the Nazi leadership to have been a huge success. The film was viewed by some twenty million Germans.

Revising German History after World War II

After Germany's defeat in 1945, the nation was occupied by the victorious Allied powers, and for four decades was divided into two distinct states. The larger and wealthier of the two, the German Federal Republic, or "West Germany," was formed from the American, British, and French occupation zones and was allied with the United States in the Cold War. The smaller state, the German Democratic Republic (DDR), or "East Germany," was formed from the Soviet occupation zone and functioned as a Soviet satellite. Until their eventual reunification in 1990, each of these German states sought to replace the Nazi historical narrative with a new history. The two states boasted different political systems and different places in the international community. Accordingly, each adopted a distinctive historical narrative and, in particular, each made certain to teach its children a version of German history that served its interests in the present.

Textbooks in the DDR viewed history from a Marxist and pro-Soviet perspective. They presented Nazism as merely an extreme form of fascism created by defenders of the obsolete capitalist system to save German monopoly capital, to subdue the German working class, and to provide German capitalists with lucrative orders for armaments in support of an imperialist enterprise.[28] Subsequently, according to this narrative, British and French capitalists sought to build up Nazi Germany in order to use it for a war against the Soviet Union. Even when it became clear that the Nazis represented a threat to the Western capitalist powers, these selfsame powers refused to join with the Soviet Union in its peacekeeping efforts. The Soviet Union was left on its own to defeat Nazi Germany, which it did. The Americans intervened toward the end of the war in order to limit Soviet influence in Western Europe. As for the Nazi Party's extreme anti-Semitism, this is given little attention or mentioned in passing as one of many examples of the ferocity of monopoly capitalists toward subject populations. Indeed, East German leaders ignored the plight of Jewish survivors, paid little attention to Israel, and purged comrades who seemed too concerned about Israel and the Jews.[29] With the end of the war, according to the official narrative, the Soviet Union sought to help Germans establish a peaceful, prosperous, and democratic state. These efforts were undermined by the Americans who built an antidemocratic outpost of imperialism and monopoly capitalism in the western portion of Germany.

East German cinema, for its part, focused on the events and legacy of the Nazi era in a series of *Trummerfilmen* (rubble films) filmed literally in the postwar rubble of bombed German cities and sought to identify the meaning or cause of the devastation.[30] Under the watchful eyes of the authorities, East German directors produced a number of films showing that Germany's predicament had been caused by industrialists and the Junker aristocracy and was now being resolved by Communism. For example, the 1949 film *Die Bunkartierten* (The Checkered Ones) tells the story of Guste, the illegitimate daughter of a house maid, born in 1884. Guste marries Paul, a factory worker who is soon sent to the front in the First World War. Waiting for Paul to return, Guste works in a munitions factory where she learns from Socialist workers that the war had been caused by industrialists seeking to profit from armaments contracts. Paul survives the war and becomes a trade union organizer. However, when the Nazis come to power, Paul is fired from his job and dies. Guste's children are all killed in a bombing raid, leaving only a surviving granddaughter. After the war, the granddaughter is able to attend an East German university where she learns the advantages of socialism and its quest for peace and freedom. The film was directed by veteran Communist filmmaker Kurt Maetzig, who produced nearly thirty films until falling out of favor with the regime in the 1970s.

The West German view of recent history was rather different from the East German account. During the early years of the Allied occupation of what would become West Germany, the U.S., in particular, discouraged the reestablishment of a German film industry and, instead, compelled theaters to show Hollywood films that were sharply critical of the recently defeated Nazi regime. As it reestablished itself, West German cinema focused on such issues as individual vs. collective guilt for the Nazi past, the guilt of ordinary Germans for wartime atrocities, and the horrors of the war. This last theme is illustrated by the 1959 film *Die Brucke* (The Bridge), which follows seven schoolboys called up for military service in the last months of the war and assigned to defend a bridge against the advancing Americans. Unlike the glorification of sacrifice in Nazi-era war films, these boys sacrifice their lives for no particular purpose.

Generally speaking, postwar German films attempt to distinguish average Germans from the nation's former Nazi leaders. Thus, the *08/15* film trilogy produced in 1954–55 portrays German soldiers as heroic victims, fighting on behalf of a regime they did not support.[31] *Des Teufels General* (The Devil's General) similarly attempts to exonerate the office corps from the crimes of the Nasi period by presenting a tale of an anti-Nazi air force general who seeks to sabotage the Nazi war effort. This rehabilitation of the German military was generally supported by American authorities who now viewed the Soviet Union as a threat against which German military support might be needed.

As to textbooks, under the watchful eyes of the occupation governments, West German histories and textbooks initially focused on "denazification," which included revising history texts to emphasize the crimes of the Nazi era. World War II was acknowledged to have been mainly, albeit not exclusively, a war of German aggression. Germany's Nazi leaders were described as thugs and criminals who committed heinous crimes against humanity. Many books published during the Nazi era were ordered destroyed and possession of one particular book, Hitler's *Mein Kampf*, which had been required reading under the Nazis, was now declared to be unlawful.

Millions of Germans had been willing participants in what were now being described as the crimes of the Nazi era. Nevertheless, history texts gradually absolved most citizens of complicity and focused on the bestiality of a small leadership cadre that had hijacked the German state and moved it in directions utterly inconsistent with the German past.[32] Even the German Federal Republic's first premier, Konrad Adenauer, who initially acknowledged the complicity of millions of ordinary Germans in the Nazi regime's crimes, soon took the position that ordinary Germans should be left in peace and not be subjected to postwar prosecutions.[33] With the Nazis safely removed from power, Germany, at least West Germany, was to resume playing a leading role in advancing European civilization.

As to East Germany, the DDR was generally portrayed in West German texts as an unwilling captive of the Soviet Union whose citizens were coerced into serving a regime that most found detestable. Germany's reunification in 1990, which generally entailed absorption of the former East Germany into the much larger and more prosperous Federal Republic, meant that the historical narrative developed in the West would now be taught in the East as well. Indeed, the Federal Republic made a determined effort to erase East German history by renaming streets, removing statutes of Marx and Lenin from public places, and assigning texts to students in the former East Germany that characterized the DDR as a totalitarian dictatorship.[34]

Since reunification, Germany has become Europe's leading industrial and commercial power and the chief beneficiary from free trade within the European Union. In some respects, Germany achieved through commerce a European dominion it failed to achieve via war. Consistent with

Germany's place at the forefront of a united Europe, German textbooks today present Germany as a committed participant in Europe and its Nazi past an unfortunate mistake not to be repeated. Nationalistic themes have been downplayed in German texts in favor of the idea of a unified and democratic Europe.[35]

Nevertheless, by the second decade of the twenty-first century, German conservative parties had decided to make use of nationalistic themes to appeal to German pride and to stiffen resistance to Muslim immigration—a bitterly contested matter throughout Western Europe and the United States. A political strategy relying upon nationalistic themes required a new look at German war crimes. After all, national guilt and national pride could not easily coexist. Hence, such groups as the Alternative for Germany (AfD) launched campaigns to change how Germans viewed their past. AfD spokespersons declared that an obsession with Nazi crimes skewed Germans' understanding of their history and left no place for national pride. It was a national obsession with the crimes of the Third Reich that led to such disastrous decisions—in the view of the German right—as the government's commitment to welcome hundreds of thousands of Muslim asylum seekers to Germany. The AfD sought to provide Germans with a "more balanced" view of history in order to change the policies of the present.[36] The AfD, for example, sought to end school trips to concentration camps in favor of visits to "significant German historic sites" where children could learn to be proud rather than ashamed of their nation's past.

Germany may be a unique case in terms of the number of times its history has been substantially revised within a short time span, but revision of national narratives, albeit less frequent and less detailed than the several histories of Germany, is commonplace. Take the example of France. After World War II, the government of President Charles de Gaulle took great pains to promote a heroic history of French resistance to the German occupiers. Until American, British, and Canadian forces landed at Normandy, however, neither the French nor the Germans had been aware of much in the way of French resistance. Asked at the Nuremberg war crimes trials about the impact of French resistance upon military production, Reich armaments minister Albert Speer seemed puzzled and said he had actually not been aware of any French resistance.[37] As historians Eric Conan and Henry Russo observe, the history of the resistance was "spruced up" by French politicians who sought to emphasize French heroism and downplay the extent to which the Vichy regime represented the views of many Frenchmen.[38]

And, of course, modern Russian history has also been spruced up several times, most recently by the Putin government. In 2007, Putin organized a conference for history teachers where he recommended that they follow a new government manual developed to sort out what he called the "muddle" in teachers' heads. The manual, "A Modern History of Russia: 1945–2006," is the basis for a series of new Russian history textbooks. The manual declares that the former Soviet Union had its problems but was, nevertheless, "an example for millions of people around the world of the best and fairest society." Stalin's dictatorship is presented as a necessary evil given the various perils in which the Soviet regime found itself. America's current anti-Russian policy is said to require a new concentration of power, presumably in Putin's hands.[39] In this way, what some have called a gangster regime is shown to be both necessary and consistent with the general flow of Russian history.

How Effective Is the Revision of History?

Most individuals' ideas about what to do in the present are, at least in part, formed by their understanding of what happened in the past. Americans whose past frame of reference is the period prior to World War II, when efforts to "appease" Hitler encouraged German aggression, are generally dubious about attempts to placate such nations as Iran and North Korea. Those, on the other hand, whose historical memories were shaped by the Vietnam War are equally dubious about confronting such regimes. If we change ideas about the past, we also change policy preferences in the present.

To demonstrate this idea empirically, we developed a survey in which respondents were asked their views about several current issues. The survey was administered to a nationally representative sample of 1,814 respondents. The survey was built using Qualtrics software and Qualtrics administered the survey online to a sample that is representative of the U.S. population with respect to age, race, and gender (based on Census proportions).

In the first set of experiments (which addressed the areas of crime, illegal immigration, health care, and violence in America), all of the respon-

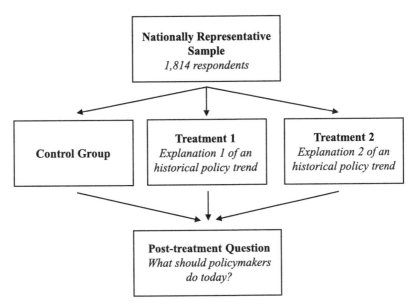

Figure 2.1. Experimental Design to Evaluate the Effect of the Past on the Present
This diagram outlines the experimental design for each policy issue. Respondents were randomly assigned to the Control, Treatment 1, or Treatment 2 group. The treatment groups were presented with different historical frames for a particular policy trend while the control group was not presented with a historical frame.

dents were randomly assigned to one of two treatment groups or a control group. The first treatment group was told one version of history relevant to a policy issue; the second treatment group was told an alternative version of history; and the third group served as a control and was not presented with any history. Immediately after the treatment (history lesson about a particular policy issue), respondents were asked about their current opinion with respect to that issue. We then compared the current policy preferences of the treatment groups to those of the untreated control group. The procedure was repeated using the same treatment and control groups for three additional policy issues. Figure 2.1 provides a graphic representation of the experimental setup for each policy area.

In another set of experiments embedded within the survey, respondents were divided into eight treatment groups and a control group to assess the relative influence of the past and future, a topic we will discuss in subsequent chapters. For the analysis at hand, we use two of these treatment

TABLE 2.1. Evidence of Random Assignment

For crime, illegal immigration, health care, and violence	Control	Treatment 1	Treatment 2
Male	44.5%	46.3%	50.7%
Age (% age 18–34)	31.0	27.8	30.8
Black	14.9	10.4	12.2
Hispanic	9.3	10.9	11.9
Income (% 0–$50K)	50.5	55.4	53.4
Education (% HS grad.)	21.3	22.2	24.2
Liberal	19.3	19.2	18.7
Moderate	43.2	42.4	41.8
Conservative	20.3	19.5	17.0
Follow government affairs	47.4	47.7	48.3
N	616	616	584
For immigration, war and peace, economy, foreign policy, and foreign terrorism			
Male	46.1%	45.2%	47.6%
Age (% age 18–34)	19.5	19.2	15.1
Black	13.9	13.9	11.2
Hispanic	7.4	11.1	10.2
Income (% 0–$50K)	53.9	53.8	49.5
Education (% HS grad.)	27.4	25.0	26.7
Liberal	29.8	27.4	30.6
Moderate	45.6	39.4	41.8
Conservative	24.7	29.8	27.7
Follow government affairs	50.2	48.6	46.1
N	215	208	206

This table presents the distribution of demographic variables for the two treatment groups and control group. HS stands for high school.

groups to test the effect of the past on the present (in the areas of immigration, war and peace, economy, foreign policy, and foreign terrorism).

Evidence of randomization for both sets of experiments is presented in table 2.1. Clearly the treatment and control groups are quite similar with respect to a range of demographics, include gender, age, race, socioeconomic status, and political engagement. We can therefore be confident that differences in response to the posttreatment questions can be attributed to the treatment.[40]

To begin with, consistent with the well-known principle of acquiescence bias, members of both treatment groups tended to express agreement with the historical account they were given (see table 2.2).[41] Decades of survey research have shown that most respondents are inclined to agree rather than disagree with an authoritative statement. Hence, as in the example below, in the group told that, historically, the American economy performed better when the government stayed out, 64 percent of the respondents agreed. On the other hand, when told that historically the economy performed better when the government intervened, more than 60 percent of respondents in a virtually identical group agreed with that statement. The full text of each treatment is given in the appendix.

Let us see how this malleability of history can affect the present. Each set of respondents, along with the control group that had not received a history "lesson," was asked about its current policy preferences on nine issues: immigration, war and peace, the economy, foreign policy, terrorism, crime, illegal immigration, health care, and violence in America. The results are quite striking. When asked, for example, whether the U.S. should invest in more border security or identify a path for undocumented immigrants to become citizens, respondents answered in a manner consistent with their answer to the first question. Those who had been told that illegal immigration had been a threat and agreed strongly favored border security (76%); those who had been told that illegal immigration had generally been good for America (and agreed) favored finding a route to citizenship (66%). The control group was much more closely divided (57% and 43%, respectively). Depending upon what history they were told, the two groups expressed preferences that differ substantially from one another and from the control group. Table 2.3 displays this phenomenon for all of the policy issues under study. It would seem that changing their understanding of history can change respondents' preferences in the present.

On average, as shown by figure 2.2, the policy preferences of those who receive a history lesson are changed 15.6 percentage points relative to untreated control groups. This substantial change seems to indicate the powerful impact of revising history upon individuals' current preferences.

It is important to address the question of whether the effects in table 2.3 and figure 2.2 are driven by ideology rather than the treatments. First, we note that several of the issues and associated treatments used in the survey do not align with a traditional liberal-conservative ideological spectrum.

TABLE 2.2. Agreement with a "History Lesson"

Policy Area	Treatments	Strongly agree/ Agree	Strongly disagree/ Disagree
Immigration	**Treatment 1:** America better off prior to recent immigration wave	57.8%	42.2%
	Treatment 2: American worse off prior to recent immigration wave	34.6%	65.4%
War and Peace	**Treatment 1:** Historically, U.S. safest when military strongest	75.8%	24.2%
	Treatment 2: Historically, U.S. safest when avoided conflicts	74.1%	25.9%
Economy	**Treatment 1:** Historically, economy better off when government stayed out	64.0%	36.0%
	Treatment 2: Historically, economy better off when government intervened	60.4%	39.6%
Foreign Policy	**Treatment 1:** Historically, U.S. has been friendly with Russia	41.2%	58.8%
	Treatment 2: Historically, U.S. has been friendly with China	66.6%	33.4%
Terrorism	**Treatment 1:** Historically, best defense has been to strike first	72.8%	27.2%
	Treatment 2: Historically, best off by maintaining good relations	66.3%	33.7%
Crime	**Treatment 1:** 1980–2010 drop in crime caused by "get tough" policies	65.3%	34.7%
	Treatment 2: 1980–2010 drop in crime caused by better education/ social services	78.7%	21.3%
Illegal Immigration	**Treatment 1:** History of illegal immigration poses a threat	65.6%	34.4%
	Treatment 2: Immigrants have contributed to growth	71.8%	28.2%
Health Care	**Treatment 1:** Rise in premiums caused by costs of medical care	85.9%	14.1%
	Treatment 2: Rise in premiums caused by fee-for-service model	77.0%	23.0%
Violence in America	**Treatment 1:** Escalation caused by lack of attention to mental illness	72.7%	27.3%
	Treatment 2: Escalation caused by weak gun laws	70.1%	29.9%

TABLE 2.3. Manipulating History to Affect Present-Day Policy Preferences

History Lesson Treatment	Support for Present-Day Policy (%)	
Crime	Strengthen mandatory minimums	Invest in support services
Treatment 1: Agree "get tough" policies caused lower crime rates	35.6	
Control	30.4	
Treatment 2: Agree more social services caused lower crime rates		84.1
Control		50.0
Illegal Immigration	Invest in border security	Help undocumented immigrants become citizens
Treatment 1: Agree immigration created a threat	76.0	
Control	56.7	
Treatment 2: Agree immigration contributed to growth		65.6
Control		43.3
Health Care	Negotiate to lower costs	Develop alternative payment model
Treatment 1: Agree rising premiums caused by high costs	66.4	
Control	68.0	
Treatment 2: Agree rising premiums caused by "fee for service"		39.5
Control		31.9
Violence	Invest in community health programs	Strengthen gun laws
Treatment 1: Agree increase in violence caused by mental illness	58.7	
Control	52.6	
Treatment 2: Agree increase in violence caused by weak gun laws		67.9
Control		47.4
Immigration	Restrict immigration	Encourage immigration
Treatment 1: Agree America better before recent immigration wave	85.5	
Control	43.5	
Treatment 2: Agree America worse before recent immigration wave		43.5
Control		38.1

TABLE 2.3—*Continued*

War and Peace	Invest in military	Work with international organizations
Treatment 1: Agree U.S. safest when military was most powerful	62.8	
Control	26.1	
Treatment 2: Agree U.S. safest when avoided conflicts		77.9
Control		73.9

Economy	Leave economy to private sector	Regulate economy more
Treatment 1: Agree U.S. better when government left economy to private sector	63.8	
Control	39.5	
Treatment 2: Agree U.S. better when government intervened in economy		74.0
Control		60.5

Foreign Policy	Improve relations with Russia	Improve relations with China
Treatment 1: Agree U.S. has been friendly with Russia	55.9	
Control	35.8	
Treatment 2: Agree U.S. has been friendly with China		69.7
Control		64.2

Foreign Terrorism	Strike terrorists first	Use diplomacy to solve problems
Treatment 1: Agree best defense against terrorism has been to strike first	61.9	
Control	48.8	
Treatment 2: Agree best defense against terrorism has been diplomacy		72.8
Control		51.2

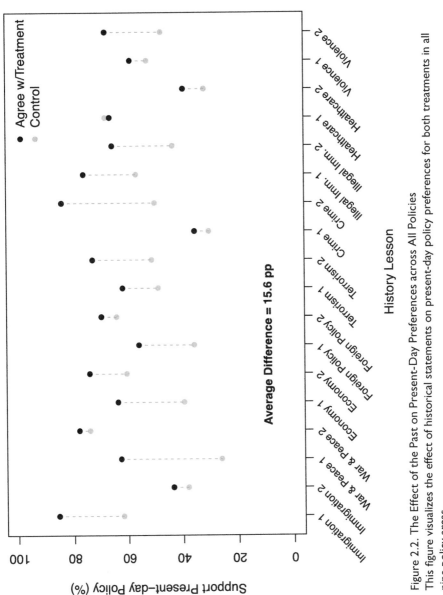

Figure 2.2. The Effect of the Past on Present-Day Preferences across All Policies
This figure visualizes the effect of historical statements on present-day policy preferences for both treatments in all nine policy areas.

For our example, the health care treatments ask whether respondents agree that the cause of rising premiums is attributable to (1) increased medical costs or (2) fee-for-service pricing. Our treatments about foreign policy ask whether respondents agree that America has generally had friendly relations with (1) China or (2) Russia. These and other treatments do not fit neatly with established liberal or conservative positions.

Nonetheless, it is certainly reasonable to expect that a respondent's prior ideology would affect their policy preferences. That said, our evidence shows that the treatments influenced preferences well above and beyond the effect of ideology. We can show this by controlling for ideology. For example, one of our treatments asked respondents whether they agree that an important cause of violence in America in recent years is (1) inadequate care for those who suffer with a mental illness or (2) weak gun laws. The first position would typically be associated with a conservative ideology and the second position with a liberal ideology. If we compare the present-day policy preference regarding how to combat violence of self-identified liberals in the control group to self-identified liberals in the "weak gun laws" treatment group, we find a statistically significant difference.[42] The same pattern emerges when we examine the issue of crime; self-identified liberals in the control group express different policy preferences than self-identified liberals in the treatment groups. In sum, we do not find that ideology is the sole driver of policy preferences; the historical lessons presented to the respondents make a meaningful difference.

To the extent that predispositions do affect respondents' policy preferences, we find that having a negative predisposition toward a particular issue exerts a stronger influence than having a positive predisposition. We return to this issue later in the chapter in our discussion about "dissidents," namely those who disagreed with the history lesson with which they were presented.

The Erasure Effect

In fictional accounts of time travel, changing the past is basically undetectable because those living in the present are unaware that they might previously have held a different understanding of the past. Our experiment reveals a similar effect. We asked respondents how long they had held the policy preference they currently expressed and, overall, an overwhelming majority claimed their preferences were long held. For example, 85 percent of respondents claimed to have held their violence in America preference for a long time and 84 percent of respondents claimed to have held their illegal immigration policy preference for a long time. This seems highly improbable as we can see by comparing the two treatment groups to the control group.

A bit of simple arithmetic can give us an estimate of this erasure effect. For each policy domain, the control group is, in effect, a pretreatment group. It represents preferences in the absence of, or prior to receipt of, the history lessons given to the treatment groups. One could say that before treatment on the issue of illegal immigration, 57 percent of respondents thought we should invest in more border security and 43 percent were in favor of a route to citizenship. Expressing agreement with a treatment, in the form of an assertion about history, as we saw in table 2.3, changed these percentages quite markedly. Among those who were told immigration had historically posed a threat (and agreed), 76 percent now favored increased border security while among those told that immigration had contributed to America's growth (and agreed), 66 percent now favored creating a path to citizenship for undocumented immigrants.

Among the members of the first treatment group who agreed with the history lesson, 87 percent claimed to have held their policy views for a long time. Thus, 87 percent of the 76 percent, equaling 66 percent of those supporting increased border security, said they had always favored this idea. However, this view was supported by only 57 percent of the demographically comparable control group. This 9 percentage point discrepancy suggests that, for at least some respondents, the effect of new knowledge about the past is to "erase" even the recollection of previous understandings. This finding is analogous to the substitution effect described by psychologist Daniel Kahneman, who noted that new beliefs could replace old ones without leaving a trace of the latter's existence.[43] In a similar vein, 87 percent of the 66 percent, equaling 57 percent of the respondents who now thought that the U.S. should create a route to citizenship for undocumented immigrants, asserted that they had always held this belief. However, this view was only supported by 43 percent of the members of the control group. Here we have a 14 percentage point discrepancy between respondents' recollections of their past beliefs and the past beliefs of a demographically comparable group of respondents. This suggests, again, an erasure of the recollection of past understandings. A similar pattern of findings emerges across nearly all the issue domains (see table 2.4).

Thus, not only is the past malleable, but at least some are unaware that

TABLE 2.4 The Erasure Effect

(1)	Treatments (2)	Aligned Present-Day Policy (3)	Among those who agreed with given history lesson, % who say they have held this policy view for a long time (4)	% in Control group who support this same policy (5)	Memory Erasure (4)-(5) (6)
Illegal Immigration	Treatment 1: History of illegal immigration poses a threat	Invest in border security measures	66.3%	56.7%	9.6 pp
	Treatment 2: Immigrants have contributed to growth	Provide a path to citizenship	56.9%	43.3%	13.6 pp
Violence	Treatment 1: Escalation caused by lack of attention to mental illness	Invest in mental health programs	51.34%	52.60%	1.3 pp
	Treatment 2: Escalation caused by weak gun laws	Pass stronger gun laws	61.76%	47.40%	14.4 pp
Immigration	Treatment 1: America better off prior to recent immigration wave	Restrict immigration	72.4%	61.9%	10.5 pp
	Treatment 2: American worse off prior to recent immigration wave	Encourage immigration	49.8%	38.1%	11.7 pp
Foreign Policy	Treatment 1: Historically, best defense has been to strike first	Strike foreign terrorists first	55.0%	48.8%	6.2 pp
	Treatment 2: Historically, best off by maintaining good relations	Use diplomacy to solve problems	61.0%	51.2%	9.8 pp
Economy	Treatment 1: Historically, economy better off when gov. stayed out	Leave economy to the private sector	49.6%	39.5%	10.1 pp
	Treatment 2: Historically, economy better off when gov. intervened	Regulate the economy more	58.6%	60.5%	-1.9 pp

Note: pp stands for percentage points

what they currently believe has been changed by a rewriting of the past. Their memories have, in effect, been erased. Governments and contending political forces correctly believe that if they can rewrite history they can alter preferences in the present and, at least in the minds of some citizens, erase even the memory of prior ideas. After rewriting historical facts, Orwell's Winston Smith had difficulty remembering what even he had previously believed. How many Americans remember what they previously believed about, say, the Russians or the Germans or the Chinese or the Japanese in the wake of concerted official efforts to frame history, shape policy preferences, and erase past understandings.

The Dissidents

For each treatment group, despite the effects of acquiescence bias, a significant percentage of respondents expressed disagreement with the history lesson that constituted their group's treatment. Among these dissidents an extremely high percentage subsequently expressed policy preferences inconsistent with the history they were told (see table 2.5). For example, those prompted to agree with the idea that immigration contributed to America's historical growth who, instead, disagreed, were the strongest of all groups in their support for more border security. Similarly, those who disagreed with the assertion that immigration had generally posed a threat to America were the strongest of all groups in their support for a path to citizenship for undocumented immigrants.

These dissidents, roughly 25 percent of all respondents, are individuals who support a particular historical narrative and react vigorously against attempts to introduce some alternative narrative. We see this in such cases as mobilization of irredentist groups in defense of Confederate statues when efforts are made to remove them from display. History is malleable, but established versions have their defenders who may not give in easily to editing and rewriting of what they view as established facts—although, of course, in the real world of government and politics "treatment" would take the form of lessons repeated frequently and over a long period of time, presumably further reducing the number of dissidents. In some times and places those who continue to dissent from official history might find themselves subject to repression. At other times and other places, dissidents might, like Scottish nationalists or Catalonian separatists, form a nucleus of support for the next revision of history.

TABLE 2.5. The Dissenters (History Lessons)

Policy Area (1)	Treatments (2)	% Disagreed with treatment (3)	Among those who disagreed, % who support a policy inconsistent with treatment (4)	% in Control group who support the same policy as those in Column 4 (5)
Crime	Treatment 1: Drop in crime caused by "get tough" policies	34.7%	85.1%	69.6%
	Treatment 2: Drop in crime caused by better education/social services	21.3%	50.0%	30.4%
Illegal Immigration	Treatment 1: History of illegal immigration poses a threat	34.4%	81.1%	43.3%
	Treatment 2: Immigrants have contributed to growth	28.2%	87.8%	56.7%
Health Care	Treatment 1: Rise in premiums caused by costs of medical care	14.1%	35.6%	32.0%
	Treatment 2: Rise in premiums caused by fee-for-service model	23.0%	64.9%	68.0%
Violence	Treatment 1: Escalation caused by lack of attention to mental illness	27.3%	54.8%	47.4%
	Treatment 2: Escalation caused by weak gun laws	29.9%	67.8%	52.6%
Immigration	Treatment 1: America better off prior to recent immigration wave	42.2%	57.0%	38.1%
	Treatment 2: American worse off prior to recent immigration wave	65.4%	66.3%	61.9%
War and Peace	Treatment 1: Historically, U.S. safest when military strongest	24.2%	94.4%	74%
	Treatment 2: Historically, U.S. safest when avoided conflicts	25.9%	36.8%	26.1%
Economy	Treatment 1: Historically, economy better off when government stayed out	36.0%	79.4%	60.5%
	Treatment 2: Historically, economy better off when government intervened	39.6%	65.8%	39.5%
Foreign Policy	Treatment 1: Historically, U.S. has been friendly with Russia	58.8%	63.4%	64.2%
	Treatment 2: Historically, U.S. has been friendly with China	33.4%	33.5%	35.8%
Terrorism	Treatment 1: Historically, best defense has been to strike first	27.2%	83.3%	51.2%
	Treatment 2: Historically, best off by maintaining good relations	33.7%	62.9%	48.8%

Note: Column 3 includes those who said they "disagree" and "strongly disagree."

Explaining Dissent

Who are the dissidents? Are they well-educated individuals who dismiss efforts to rewrite history? An investigation of which factors drive dissent reveals that political ideology, above all else, is the most influential. Figure 2.3 compares the effect of ideology, education, and political engagement on respondents' likelihood of disagreeing with the history lesson presented to them.[44] As is evident in the figure, the effect of ideology far exceeds the effect of education and political engagement (two well-documented determinants of political opinion). Note that the graph plots the effect of self-defining oneself as a liberal or strong liberal; the effects of self-defining oneself as a conservative or strong conservative would have the same strength but in the opposite direction. It seems that efforts to rewrite history are most likely to be rejected by those whose credenda—not knowledge—cause them to reject new ideas. These ideologues, in fact, react negatively to efforts to teach them new versions of events and rush to affirm their support for policies inconsistent with the history now being foisted upon them.

The Unsettled Past

Efforts to revise history, whether through textbooks or films, or even the Orwellian memory holes approximated by the North Korean government, are not always conclusive. The old history has its defenders and can leave artifacts attesting to the former reality. These include languages, monuments, and even funerary artifacts as in the case of the Incas. Proponents of the new history may need to work for decades or even centuries to destroy the artifactual record of the old history. Sometimes an old history is, nevertheless, restored as in the modern-day cases of Catalonia and Scotland where the preservation of a language provided a portal into an almost-forgotten past and made this past available to new political forces in the present era.

Interestingly, but perhaps not surprisingly, it is the ideologues, or true believers, not the well educated, who are most likely to resist historical revisionism and cling to their established memories. This observation seems consistent with the difficulties government face when attempting to reeducate "fanatical" Nazis or "hard-core" Confederate sympathizers. Such individuals, clinging tenaciously to an about-to-be forgotten past, sometimes open the way for its recollection and reassertion.

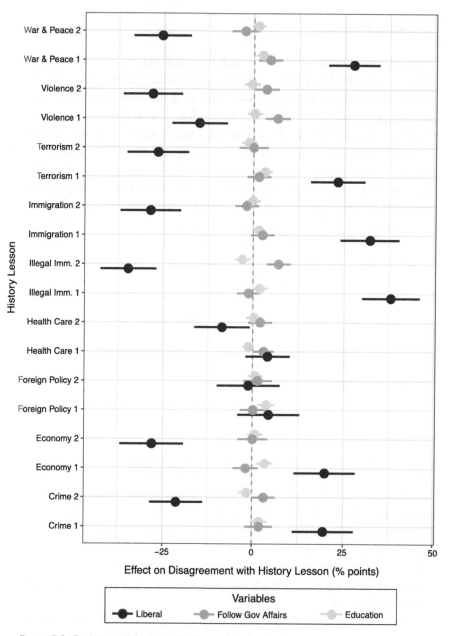

Figure 2.3. Explaining Dissent with History Lessons
This graph compares the effect of ideology, education, and political engagement
(measured as the extent to which respondents follow government affairs) on
respondents' likelihood of disagreeing with the history lesson presented to them. The
results show that the effect of ideology is strongest across nearly all policy areas.

CHAPTER 3

Reimagining the Future to Reshape the Present

From a Newtonian perspective, past, present, and future follow a regular sequence with the future always last in causal order. This is the basis for the familiar idea of the arrow of time that flies in only one direction. Yet, as we observed in chapters 1 and 2, the passage of time is not quite so simple nor is it necessarily unilinear. Events in the present can affect accounts of the past in ways that reverberate back into the present where they materialize in the form of action. And, as we shall see, ideas about the future often affect the present where they can also materialize into actions that, in turn, help to shape the future. In essence, past, future, and present are locked in a complex embrace that does not precisely follow Newtonian pathways. This embrace, as we saw in chapter 1, provides contending political forces with the opportunity to alter the present by reimagining the future.

If we consider the possible relationships between present and future, we should certainly acknowledge that events in the present affect the future. Indeed, at least according to one interpretation of quantum theory, events in the present create an infinite number of futures.[1] As we observed in chapter 1, however, many, if not most, of the actions undertaken in the present are, themselves, influenced by individuals' expectations about the future. What individuals wear, or their plans for the day, are often based upon the weather forecast. Families purchase insurance policies to protect themselves from the potential consequences of future mishaps. Insurers price this insurance on the basis of the estimated future probability that the mishap will occur. Workers invest funds for their future retirement in financial instruments they hope will provide the largest future return. Indeed, the future expectations of workers, employers, and investors have become major components of most macroeconomic models. In these and numerous other ways, ideas about the future shape and even dominate actions in the present.

Beyond the immediate effects of expectations upon behavior, the future shapes the present in a number of fundamental ways. In science fiction films, as we observed in chapter 1, individuals travel into the future and encounter concepts or scientific discoveries that they can use in the present. Alternatively, travelers from the future arrive in the present bearing technologies with the potential to alter both the present and future. While such notions are treated as imaginative fiction, they contain more than a kernel of truth. Not only is knowledge routinely retrieved from the future, at least in the form of probabilities, but, as in science fiction, this knowledge from the future and the theories and techniques employed to collect it can produce a variety of spin-offs. Indeed, interest in the future has prompted civilizations in the past and present to develop three basic tools. These are scientific inquiry, the capacity to plan, and the construction of instruments and techniques with which to change the future.

As to the first of these tools, science fiction films are not far off the mark when they depict scientific ideas and inventions being brought back from the future. Viewed from a particular perspective, science is a product of the future. Consider that the chief purpose of scientific research is prediction, and it was concern about the future that prompted the development of a variety of modes of investigation that promised to predict future events. Some of these forms of inquiry, to be sure, including astrology, divination, crystal gazing, and so forth, turned out not to be very reliable. These were gradually replaced by practices that offered more accurate forecasts. These included astronomy, meteorology, climatology, polling, macroeconomic forecasting, and other scientific methods. In this way, the future has continually served as a wellspring of scientific discovery by validating scientific methods while discrediting pseudoscience and fakery. This is why science fiction films in which knowledge is brought back from the future are not so very wrong.

The process of information transfer from the future to the present is seldom as dramatic as its depiction in science fiction films. Such transfers are not accompanied by the flashes of light and crackles of energy that marked, say, the Terminator's arrival from the future. Nevertheless, information about likely future events continually shapes present-day thought and action. Take, for example, weather forecasting.

Ability to anticipate changes in the weather is crucial to agriculture, navigation, military campaigns, commerce, and to a host of other human activities that are vulnerable to disruption by adverse weather conditions. As a result, records of efforts to forecast future weather date back at least four millennia. Ancient Egyptian, Chinese, and Indian astronomers developed methods, albeit not very accurate ones, for predicting the weather, the Babylonians studied cloud formations to forecast the weather, and Aristotle developed an extensive analysis of weather patterns and very likely coined the term "meteorology" to describe the science of weather forecasting.

Aristotle understood that weather systems generally move downwind so that knowing the weather upwind is generally a good predictor of the near-term future weather for any given location. This knowledge, though, offered little help in forecasting the weather until humans were able to develop systems able to transmit information over relatively long distances at a speed faster than the movement of weather systems. This capacity came with the invention of the telegraph in the 1830s. Telegraphy came to be used widely during the 1840s to provide downwind locations with weather reports, thus giving them a peek of as much as several days into the meteorological future. During the 1860s, the British Board of Trade established a series of telegraph stations to provide daily weather reports and forecasts, including storm warnings for areas hundreds of miles, and hence days, downwind. Over the ensuing decades, efforts to produce more reliable and longer-range weather forecasts helped to stimulate advances in computer modeling as well as innovations in such fields as atmospheric dynamics, fluid dynamics, and applied mathematics whose importance goes beyond weather forecasting.

Every day, a great deal of knowledge from the meteorological future is collected and put to use. Farmers use weather forecasts to determine what crops to plant, when to harvest crops, and where to plant their crops. Airlines and shipping companies use weather forecasts to plan their routes and schedules. Utility companies use weather forecasts to anticipate power demand. Military planners use weather forecasts to guide their tactics. In these ways, knowledge obtained from the future has important consequences for the present, and, for its part, learning to collect and analyze this information from the future has promoted inquiry and technology in a number of present-day fields.

As we observed in chapter 1, another realm in which the impact of the future on the present has been studied carefully is macroeconomics. Most macroeconomic models have incorporated the future expectations of consumers and other economic decision-makers when making decisions about such issues as consumption, investment, and pricing.[2]

Voters are also cognizant of the future and take account of candidates' electoral chances when casting votes. One of the best-known examples of this idea is sometimes called fear of the "lost vote," which tends to gradually reduce the number of parties that compete for power in some nations. In nations like the United States, whose voting rules award few or no legislative seats to minor parties, supporters of independent candidates or minor parties, expecting their preferred choice to lose, will tend to cast their ballots for the least objectionable of the major party candidates. Voters' fear of wasting their votes is one reason that third-party candidates seldom do well in the U.S. and that the two-party system has remained intact. In this way, future expectations protect an important aspect of current political reality.

Planning for the Future

With what is at least thought to be reliable information about the future, as suggested by the examples above, comes the capacity to make rational plans. Successful planning requires reasonably accurate information about events likely to occur in the future. The possession of such information, be it meteorological or other knowledge about future occurrences and possibilities, opens the way for planning to mitigate or, perhaps, even benefit from the consequences of the events that have been foreseen. The more accurate the foreknowledge, the greater the likelihood of a successful plan. One of the first known examples of planning based upon a forecast, albeit a forecast of questionable validity, is given by the Hebrew Bible. In the book of Exodus, Joseph sees into the future through his interpretation of the Pharaoh's dream. Joseph foresees seven years of plenty followed by seven years of famine. Armed with this information, Joseph advises the Pharaoh to store 20 percent of the grain harvested during each of the next seven years to avert starvation during the ensuing seven. Whether the biblical account is exactly right or not, it seems clear that as long ago as the

Hyksos period (1800 B.C.), the Egyptians were, indeed, seeking to forecast droughts and to plan accordingly if one was thought to be in the offing.[3]

One great impetus for planning has always been military exigency. Most states—at least those that survived—learned that before going to war it was wise to look to the future by estimating their own revenues and resources over the coming years while gathering information about their enemies' strengths and future plans. Based upon this information, military tacticians could devise plans for successful campaigns. The Hebrew Bible, again, offers an excellent example. In the book of Numbers, before sending his forces across the Jordan River to invade Canaan, Moses conducts a census to determine how many soldiers the Hebrews might be able to muster and sends twelve spies to determine the strength of the forces they are likely to encounter. Based upon the reports filed by the spies and the results of the census, most Hebrews, albeit not including Moses himself, conclude that it would be better to wait and increase their numbers to make the balance of forces more favorable to the Hebrew cause. The invasion of Canaan was delayed for some years until a new generation of soldiers could be produced and trained, but the result was a successful military conquest of the Promised Land. This biblical account is one of the earliest recorded examples of a military plan based upon a projection into the future.

All successful ancient empires learned to collect intelligence and use it to engage in extensive planning for their military campaigns. Sun Tzu, a sixth-century B.C. Chinese general, discussed the importance of planning in the first of the thirteen chapters of *The Art of War*: "The general who loses a battle makes but few calculations beforehand. Thus do many calculations lead to victory, and few calculations to defeat: how much more no calculation at all! It is by attention to this point that I can see who is likely to win or lose."[4] Several centuries later, Niccolò Machiavelli wrote, "Men who have any great undertaking in mind must first make all necessary preparations for it, so that, when an opportunity arises, they may be ready to put it in execution according to their design."[5]

Planning began mainly as a military practice but has evolved into a standard function in civilian agencies and private firms. Entrepreneurs might once have consulted soothsayers before launching an enterprise. Today, government officials and the heads of large enterprises are more likely to use such predictive tools as macroeconomic forecasting as the

basis for strategic plans that more or less parallel those of military organizations. The notion of using military-style strategic planning for civilian
purposes is also evident in the concept of the policy institute or "think
tank." These are private institutions in the U.S. as well as a number of
other nations that engage in policy research and planning with civilian as
well as military applications. Often, the research is supported by government contracts. In Britain, the Centre for Strategic Research and Analysis
undertakes both military and civilian planning for the British government.
In the United States, similar functions are performed by the Hoover Institution, the Council on Foreign Relations, the Brookings Institution, and
a host of other enterprises that make policy recommendations on the basis
of forecasts of future threats, trends, and possibilities.

Planning for the future has numerous spillover effects that can subtly
but substantially alter the present. Take the example of the aptly named
"futures" contract, generally known as a "future." Futures allow buyers and
sellers to agree on a current price for a specified quantity of some commodity to be delivered months or years in the future. The central purpose
of the future is to allow firms to lock in the prices of, say, agricultural
commodities or other raw materials and thereby to mitigate the risk of
future price increases. The contracts, themselves, can be bought and sold
on several general and specialized exchanges such as the Chicago Board
of Trade or the Minneapolis Grain Exchange. A variety of mathematical
models are used to predict the future values of these contracts and, hence,
their current pricing.

Futures have markedly altered commodities production in the present. For buyers to agree to accept future delivery of some commodity,
they must have some assurance of the character and quality of a product
that they may not see for several years. Moreover, futures transactions on
a large scale require buyers and sellers to share common definitions of
the commodities in question. The result is that trading futures has generated ever-increasing standardization in the present. Roosevelt Institute fellow Michael Konczal offers the example of livestock futures.[6] To trade yet
unborn cattle on an exchange in the form of futures, sellers must agree that
the cattle they eventually deliver will fall within various height, weight,
and quality parameters. The exchange assures buyers of this fact so that
they will be willing to enter into the transaction. The result, over time, has
been to impose breeding, feeding, housing, and overall product standardization upon the cattle industry. The same has been true in other industries

such as dairy products and lumber. In essence, the demands of the future have substantially reorganized the present.

Such examples can be found in many realms. For instance, Americans spend more than $1 trillion per year on life, health, property, and casualty insurance in the hope of mitigating future harm.[7] Insurance companies, for their part, require the insured to adhere to a number of rules in exchange for the right to purchase coverage. Cigarette smokers, for example, can be charged a higher rate for health insurance coverage. Purchasers of auto insurance must demonstrate safe driving practices. Fire insurers insist on adherence to various fire codes. Homeowners may be told that possession of certain breeds of dogs will make them ineligible for liability insurance. In all these ways, planning to mitigate future harm can change the present.

Similarly, anticipation of future benefits from government-sponsored pension schemes, like America's Social Security system, have substantial consequences for workers' behavior in the present, including a reduction in marriage and fertility rates.[8] Assured of income in the future, workers have less incentive to marry and produce offspring whom they might have required for support in the absence of a pension system. The founder of national pensions, Germany's Otto von Bismarck, was convinced also that the promise of a future benefit would ensure workers' loyalty to the government in the present. One of America's founders, Alexander Hamilton, thought government bonds would have a similar effect. Hamilton saw government-issued bonds, which are essentially promises of future payment by the government to its creditors, as an important source of government power in the present. Hamilton believed that government bondholders would have a stake in the success of the new Union and would work in the present to make certain that their funds would be safe in the future.

Changing the Future

It is only a small step from planning to cope with or mitigate the effects of future events to endeavoring to actually change the future. Information about the future is the key to both. Information about the probability of floods, for example, might lead to evacuation planning or, perhaps, to the construction of flood control systems. The first strategy seeks to deal with the consequences of future events while the second seeks to actually change the future and prevent floods. In some cultures, efforts to change the future involve prayers or magical incantations. Others rely more heavily on science and engineering. Take, for example, the massive systems of dikes and levees along America's Mississippi River designed to prevent the river from periodically overflowing its banks as would be normal for the Mississippi's floodplain, and efforts to reduce the greenhouse gas emissions contributing to the potentially disastrous warming of the Earth's climate. Some have argued for the development of systems to warn of and destroy large asteroids that might some day strike the Earth with devastating consequences as has occurred in the past.

Of course, changing the future is fraught with risk and the potential for unforeseen adverse consequences. America's Mississippi flood control system is an example of the risks of attempting to reengineer the future. An unforeseen consequence of the construction of levees to prevent the river from inundating its floodplain has been more severe and frequent flooding along the length of the waterway as the river is prevented from slowly spreading into its normal lowlands. Prayers and incantations might have done less harm.

We should also note that, as in the case of planning, changing the future can require major changes in the present. Take the often-invoked example of world peace. Everyone from presidential candidates to beauty pageant contestants is fond of declaring that they hope to bring about a peaceful future. Yet consider what efforts might be required in the present to ensure future peace. In the political science literature there seem to be two main schools of thought regarding this matter, the Hobbesian and the Kantian schools. For Thomas Hobbes, the solution to the problem of war was the creation of a powerful sovereign authority that would put an end to strife and violent conflict.[9] For Immanuel Kant, the solution was an increase in the number of republican governments, a type of regime that, in his view, was extremely reluctant to engage in acts of armed aggression.[10] Thus, modern-day neo-Hobbesians favor the construction of supranational organizations and the dilution of national sovereignty while modern-day neo-Kantians count upon the spread of liberal democracy to bring about a "democratic peace."

The main problem faced by the neo-Hobbesians is that the establishment and maintenance of a sovereign powerful enough to suppress violence is most likely to be accepted by states or other actors that already have few or relatively manageable antagonisms toward one another and see submission to a single authority as a means of advancing their mutual interests. The thirteen American states in 1789 or the economically advanced Western European states today are examples. The imposition of some sort of sovereign authority over mutually antagonistic states and political forces would seem likely to require considerable violence and a continuing regime of coercion. In other words, it would entail an imperial project that seems more a recipe than a cure for violence. As to the neo-Kantians, America has justified many of its wars, including the 2002 Iraq War, with the claim that its goal was to transform its adversary into a peaceful liberal democracy. This suggests that Kant's vision of a peaceful future might require a good deal of bloodshed in the present to compel unwilling states to become peaceful liberal democracies in the future.

The point here is not to debunk Hobbes or Kant but, rather, to underscore the proposition that efforts to change the future can have enormous implications for the present. Whether or not the future turns out to be malleable, efforts to change the future are almost certain to change the present. In this way, too, the future dominates the present.

Defining Alternative Futures

Precisely because the future exerts a great deal of power over the present, competing forces constantly struggle to exercise influence in the present by shaping future hopes and expectations and seeking to identify themselves with desirable futures and their opponents with unattractive future possibilities. For this purpose, competing forces use a variety of instruments including scientific prediction. For example, the study of climate change documents the impact of greenhouse gas emissions from the use of fossil fuels upon the Earth's climate. The impact includes global warming, rising sea levels, and threats to the existence of many plant and animal species. In the United States, this area of scientific inquiry is strongly supported by Democrats/progressives and questioned by Republicans/conservatives. Progressives see avoidance of climate change as necessitating an increase in the power of national and international political institutions and the imposition of strict limits upon market-driven decision-making. Efforts designed to mitigate climate change have generated international agreements and volumes of rules and regulations that expand governmental reach over the national and international economy.

From the liberal perspective, climate change and the vision of the future it adduces help to drive a political agenda that liberals also find helpful for a variety of other reasons. For example, Democratic efforts to enact the wide-ranging "Build Back Better" legislation in 2021 included not only a tax incentive for the purchase of electric vehicles, but an *enhanced* tax incentive for the purchase of such vehicles when produced by union labor. Conservatives, for their part, see the same implications and question the validity of the scientific prediction in some measure because they oppose the expansion of state power and other present-day implications of the future predicted by the studies.

In a similar vein, many American conservatives assert that continued budget deficits will eventually bankrupt the nation and undermine America's standing in the world. A number of conservative groups have gone so far as to call for a "convention of the states" to rewrite the American Constitution to outlaw deficit spending. The economics of deficits are complex but the politics of deficit spending seem quite simple. Conservatives oppose deficit spending insofar as deficits allow the expansion of social programs and the concomitant growth of government control over the economy. Their dire predictions regarding the future effects of deficits are, in part, driven by a particular understanding of the present-day political significance of deficit spending (and thus they attach far less concern to certain deficit-enhancing policies such as tax cuts). Liberals generally share the understanding that deficit-mindedness can restrict the growth of government-funded programs and so generally underplay (or in the case of modern monetary theory, simply deny) any harmful future economic forecasts resulting from increased deficits. Thus, alternative visions of the future are, as is so often the case, designed to produce differing policy outcomes in the present.

Religious Visions

In large parts of the world, science has not supplanted religion as a source of prophecy. Religions offer a set of predictions about the future that often have important implications for the distribution of political power in the present. Religious forces that offer the most convincing accounts of the future are likely to gain adherents and dominate the present. Lest this idea seem confined to battles between rival Middle Eastern groups wielding alternative interpretations of Islam, let us consider the battle between America's evangelical and mainstream Protestants. Though this battle has not involved the use of much violence it is, nevertheless, an excellent example of the way in which competing visions of the future can affect the present, empowering some groups while undermining others. Since few readers will be familiar with these events, some background and detail are necessary.

In the late years of the nineteenth century, a de facto schism developed among America's Protestant churches. The mainline denominations of the Northeast, including the Methodists, Episcopalians, Presbyterians, and Congregationalists, came under the control of liberal theologians who sought to bring about a reconciliation between the Gospel and modern secular society. This reconciliation included acceptance of scientific theories such as evolution and a concern for ameliorating such social ills as poverty and inequality through the "Social Gospel," which called for the application of Christian principles to the problems and conflicts of industrial society. For liberal Protestants, the Bible was often to be understood metaphorically and salvation was not a final reward in the afterlife but a lifelong process of growth in love, service, and well-being.[11]

The churches and Bible colleges of the South and Southwest, on the other hand, were dominated by a different group of Protestants. These were the so-called fundamentalists, named for a series of pamphlets published by a group of conservative theologians early in the twentieth century and entitled *The Fundamentals: A Testimony of Truth*. In these pamphlets, which were distributed and widely read in the South, conservative pastors defended traditional Christian views, called for a literal reading of the Bible, and attacked Social Gospel advocates for presuming that salvation could be achieved through "works" rather than faith alone.

Before the Second World War, liberals and fundamentalists each dominated a discrete region of the country and ruled separate empires of churches, seminaries, and publishing houses. The two groups had serious spiritual disagreements but little direct contact. After the war, however, the liberals and fundamentalists entered into head-to-head competition in one another's territorial bastions. To begin with, during the war, large numbers of White southerners migrated from their home region to California and the upper Midwest to work in factories and defense plants. These transplanted southerners were uncomfortable in the Protestant churches—to say nothing of the secular culture—they found outside Dixie and welcomed visits from conservative ministers from their home states. These visits soon became large-scale revival meetings and crusades in which the old-time religion was preached to the faithful and the curious.

Southern California, which had been a focal point of immigration from the lower South, hosted a number of crusades in the 1940s and 1950s featuring such ministers as Billy Graham and "Fighting" Bob Shuler.[12] Graham and some of the other crusaders had already begun to call themselves evangelicals rather than fundamentalists to signal that their goal was to restore the primacy of the Gospel in a secular and sinful society. During the war, they founded the National Association of Evangelicals, which drew its membership from Pentecostals as well as fundamentalists.[13] These evangelicals built churches and religious organizations throughout the North and sought to broaden their membership base through evangelical outreach activities such as radio and television ministries, heavily publicized crusades and revivals, and organizations such as the Campus Crusade for Christ. The upshot of these efforts was that the evangelicals were soon locked in competition with the various liberal Protestant denominations on the latter's home turf.

On the heels of this southern conservative Protestant invasion of the North, northern liberal Protestantism invaded the South. During the 1960s, prominent liberal northern ministers such as Eugene Carson Blake and William Sloan Coffin joined demonstrations and protest marches and castigated their southern counterparts for failing to raise their own voices against an unjust and un-Christian apartheid system.[14] Southern Protestants were infuriated by the northern ministers' interference and accusations. Reverend Jerry Falwell first achieved national prominence with a 1965 sermon entitled "Marchers and Ministers" in which he attacked liberal Protestant ministers for intruding into southern society. The duty of the church, said Falwell, was to "preach the word," not to "reform the externals."[15]

Liberal Protestants also expanded their denominational reach through the mass media. Liberal Protestants had accepted the cultural revolution of the 1960s; indeed, they had embraced it. The major liberal denominations, along with their umbrella group, the National Council of Churches, came to support abortion rights, an end to local moral codes, racial and gender equality, limits on religious displays and symbols in public places, and, broadly, the evolution of a more secular society. In numerous films, television series, and documentaries produced in the 1950s and 1960s the ideas and sometimes the personalities of the liberal Protestants were presented in a favorable light—*A Man Called Peter*, for example, was the biography of a wise and sensitive Presbyterian minister—while the fundamentalists and evangelicals were depicted as racist, Neanderthal "bible thumpers," often venal, alcoholic, and committed to outmoded and discredited ideas. This genre includes such films as *Inherit the Wind*, a fictionalized account of the Scopes trial, and *Elmer Gantry*, the story of a drunken and dishonest Pentecostal preacher, patterned on the revivalist Billy Sunday.

If Hollywood needed encouragement to produce such films, the National Council of Churches was ready to provide it. Between the war and the late 1960s, the National Council of Churches maintained a Protestant Film Commission in Hollywood, ostensibly to encourage the production of films that promoted Christian values. For the most part, the commission encouraged the making of films that espoused the values of liberal Protestantism. For example, films that received awards from the commission in the 1960s generally were those that criticized segregation and promoted racial equality. Thus, award winners included *A Patch of Blue*, the story of a love affair between a Black man and a blind White woman, and *In the Heat of the Night*, a film in which a Black northern police officer gradually wins the respect of a bigoted White southern sheriff.

Evangelicals responded vigorously to this northern assault on their social and religious institutions, making use of both politics and religious doctrine. On the political front, between the 1960s and the 1980s evangelical ministers and activists organized such groups as the Moral Majority, the Christian Coalition, Focus on the Family, and a host of others to battle on behalf of school prayer, against abortion, against the Equal Rights Amendment, against same-sex marriage, and, generally, to halt America's "moral decline." Republican politicians, beginning with Ronald Reagan, viewed evangelicals as an important new GOP constituency and made major efforts to reach out to them through campaigns emphasizing "family values."

At the same time, evangelicals launched a major doctrinal attack on the liberal Protestants, highlighting the failure of the mainline denominations to defend the Bible against the encroachment of secularism. While the liberals preached personal growth, social justice, and self-realization through service to society, evangelicals preached faith in the Gospel and salvation through a commitment to Jesus Christ. In particular, evangelicals preached premillennialism and premillennial dispensationalism——powerful visions of the future that helped to reshape the politics of the present.

Premillennial Dispensationalism

Premillennial dispensationalism is a set of beliefs first popularized by nineteenth-century British evangelist John Nelson Darby who averred that his close reading of the Holy Scripture revealed that the return of the Jews to the Holy Land would set into motion a series of events leading to the Second Coming of Christ. Darby wrote and spoke extensively in England and America where he built a following among pastors, Bible teachers, and revivalists.[16] Darby's ideas, particularly those relating to the importance of the Jews, have had a major impact upon the views of generations of evangelical Protestants.[17] Today, dispensationalism is promoted by a network of churches and institutes and such publications as the *Scofield Reference Bible*, first published in 1909. Many aspects of dispensationalist doctrine, especially those relating to the importance of the Jews in "end times," have spread well beyond the core of adherents into the more general evangelical community including Pentecostals.

Dispensationalists divide the history of the world into seven epochs, called dispensations, beginning with the Garden of Eden. Most dispensationalists believe that we are currently living in the sixth epoch, the age of the Church, and will soon enter the seventh dispensation, the Millennial Kingdom or Millennium, a thousand-year reign of Christ on earth. Among dispensationalists, the details are disputed, but in general terms, sometime prior to the Millennium faithful Christians will ascend to the clouds in an event called the Rapture. While these true believers are safe with Jesus, the Antichrist will rule on earth for seven years. Apostates and unbelievers, including the Jews, left behind on earth will suffer terribly during this period of tribulation.

At first, the Antichrist will present himself as a benevolent dictator and will allow the Jews to rebuild the Temple of Solomon. During the fourth year of his reign, however, the Antichrist will reveal himself, persecute the Jews, outlaw the Jewish religion, and demand to be worshiped as God. When the Jews refuse, he will lead armies against Israel. Most of the Jews will be killed and the remainder will accept Christ. At this point, Christ and the raptured believers will return to earth and, in the battle of Armageddon near Jerusalem, defeat the Antichrist and his armies. The Antichrist and his followers will be thrown into a lake of fire and Satan will be chained and thrown into a bottomless pit. God will gather the nations of the earth for judgment in the Valley of Jehoshaphat where they will be judged on how they have treated God's chosen people—the Jews. After the destruction of the Antichrist and the judgment of the nations, Jesus will restore the throne of David and rule the world for one thousand years. At the end of this period, Satan will launch another rebellion, which God will suppress. This will be followed by the Day of Judgment, the resurrection of the dead, and the creation of a new heaven and a new earth.[18]

Many of these prophecies have been popularized in such best-selling books as Hal Lindsey's *The Late Great Planet Earth* and Tim LaHaye's "Left Behind" series, which has sold more than 60 million copies and served as the basis for film and television productions as well as tapes and assorted items of clothing, curios, and knickknacks. In LaHaye's stories, after the sudden rapture of millions of Bible-believing Christians, ordinary people are left behind to suffer through the seven years of tribulation. Some, albeit belatedly, repentant individuals, led by the hero, airline pilot Rayford Steele, form a "tribulation force" to resist the Antichrist who turns out to be Nicolae Carpathia, the charismatic new Romanian secretary-general of the United Nations, a pro-abortion, one-world ecumenicist. Many battles are fought and treacheries, plagues, and disasters overcome. Eventually Christ appears on a white horse leading his raptured followers to defeat the forces of darkness.

Controlling the Present with a Vision of the Future

The premillennial vision of the future became a decisive factor in what amounted to an evangelical victory over mainstream Protestants in the religious politics of the present. When Darby developed his notion of premillennial dispensationalism at the end of the nineteenth century it was welcomed by a small number of conservative theologians as a defense of biblical literalism and a powerful argument against advocates of the Social Gospel. Premillennialism declares that the conditions for the Messiah's return and human salvation are foretold in biblical prophecy and are not subject to human will. It, thus, offers a direct refutation of the liberal view that salvation is at least partially a result of good works.

Initially, though, premillennialism was something of a fringe theology, mainly popular among the tent-show revivalists who went from town to town in rural areas, primarily in the South and Southwest. These revivalists soon found that premillennialism was a crowd pleaser. The revivalists were early "masters of mass communication" and sought to appeal to people's "hopes, fears and resentments."[19] They saw in premillennialism a clear and powerful doctrine that could be understood by their audiences. While the rural folks attending a tent meeting might not catch all the subtleties of theological disputation, they could certainly understand the Rapture, the tribulation, the Second Coming, Armageddon, the fiery lake, and the other dramatic elements of the premillennialists' biblical story.

As historian Timothy Weber puts it, revivalists preaching premillennialism "out-Bibled" the competition.[20] And as preachers observed the success of their colleagues making use of premillennialist doctrines, they followed suit. As one minister put it, "I do not mean to say that the apparent outstanding success of these godly men became conclusive. . . . But it did do this for me—it started me again to study my Bible."[21] Some preached dispensationalism, with its division of history into seven periods, while others preached related forms of premillennialism.

By the Second World War, premillennialism had moved from the fringes to the evangelical mainstream. Most evangelical pastors were now premillennialists and quite a few were full-fledged dispensationalists. As the evangelicals moved North and engaged in head-to-head competition with the mainline Protestant denominations, premillennialism proved as powerful a force as it had been fifty years earlier in the South and Southwest. Mainline Protestant ministers offered their congregants the thin gruel of a doctrine of personal growth and affirmation not so different from the ideas that could be found in any secular self-help treatise. The evangelicals, on the other hand, offered fire and brimstone, rapture, and tribulation. And, with the birth of Israel, they could point out that their truth was true.

The battle between premillennialism and the Social Gospel turned out to be an unequal contest. In the 1940s, a majority of America's Protestants belonged to the mainline liberal denominations. Today, the evangelicals outnumber their rivals by a 2–1 margin. A powerful vision of the future has helped to determine the outcome of a battle in the present.

Evangelical Support for Israel

The evangelical view of the future also explains why most evangelicals strongly support Israel in the present. Israel and the Jewish people play a critical role in dispensationalist eschatology. The return of the Jews to the

Holy Land and the reestablishment of the biblical Jewish kingdom is a precondition for the emergence of the Antichrist, the period of tribulation, the battle of Armageddon, and the eventual Millennium. In the dispensationalist view, the current era is merely a "parenthesis," or interruption in God's relationship with the Jews. Those Jews who survive the time of tribulation and accept Christ as their messiah will be saved and Jesus will reign over the earth from Israel.

For evangelicals the creation and continued existence of the State of Israel is empirical proof of the truth and power of their reading of the Bible. The rebirth of Israel seems to demonstrate the superiority of evangelical doctrine to the covenantalist, postmillennialist, and other scriptural interpretations proffered by the mainline Protestants with whom evangelicals engage not only in spiritual competition but also in earthly competition for influence and adherents. Their religious beliefs tell evangelicals to support Israel and, in turn, Israel is a sign for all to see that evangelicals' religious beliefs are valid. Evangelicals have used their powerful vision of the future to enhance their influence and reshape the politics of the present.

Changing the Present by Changing the Future: Some Experimental Evidence

Using an experimental design similar to the one employed in chapter 2, we show quantitatively that altering individuals' beliefs about the future is likely to have a significant effect upon their political perspectives and preferences in the present. To demonstrate this idea empirically, we developed and employed the same Qualtrics survey described in the previous chapter. The survey was, as readers will recall, administered to a nationally representative sample of 1,814 respondents.[22]

In our experiments, which addressed the areas of immigration, national security, government regulation, relations with China and Russia, terrorism, climate change, American military strength, and the national debt, all of the respondents were randomly assigned to one of two treatment groups or to a control group. The first treatment group was given one future forecast relevant to each policy issue; the second treatment group was given an alternative forecast relevant to the same issues; and the third group served as a control and was not presented with any forecast. Immediately after each treatment (forecast), respondents were asked about their

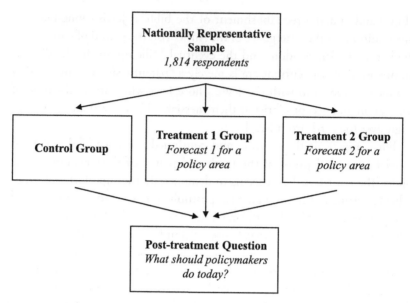

Figure 3.1. Experimental Design to Evaluate the Effect of the Future on the Present
This diagram outlines the experimental design for each policy issue. Respondents
were randomly assigned to the Control, Treatment 1, or Treatment 2 group. The
treatment groups were presented with different future forecasts about a particular
policy trend while the control group was not presented with a forecast.

current opinion with respect to that issue. We then compared the current
policy preferences of the treatment groups to those of the control group.
Figure 3.1 provides a graphic representation of the experimental setup for
each policy area.

To begin with, consistent with the principle of acquiescence bias, members of all but two of the sixteen treatment groups tended to express agreement with the forecast they were given.[23] As noted in chapter 2, decades
of survey research have shown that most respondents are inclined to agree
rather than disagree with an authoritative statement. Hence, in the group
told that nations whose governments reduced economic regulation would
be better off in the future, 61.6 percent of the respondents agreed (see
table 3.1). On the other hand, when told that nations whose governments
increased economic regulation would be better off in the future, 95 percent of respondents in a virtually identical group (demographically) agreed
with that forecast. The full text of each treatment is given in the appendix.

Let us see how changes in beliefs about the future can affect prefer-

TABLE 3.1. Agreement with a Future Forecast

Policy Area	Treatments	Strongly agree/ Agree	Strongly disagree/ Disagree
Immigration	**Treatment 1:** Immigration restrictions will make America better	75.2%	24.8%
	Treatment 2: Immigration restrictions will make America worse	45.5%	54.5%
National Security	**Treatment 1:** U.S. will be safer if it increases military strength in future	69.1%	30.9%
	Treatment 2: U.S. will be safer with more international cooperation in future	86.7%	13.3%
Economy	**Treatment 1:** Nations whose governments reduce regulations will be better off	61.6%	38.4%
	Treatment 2: Nations whose governments increase regulations will be better off	95.0%	5.0%
Foreign Policy	**Treatment 1:** Greatest threat to America will come from China in the future	56.4%	43.6%
	Treatment 2: Greatest threat to America will come from Russia in the future	51.7%	48.3%
Terrorism	**Treatment 1:** Likely terrorists will attack America in next decade	90.1%	9.9%
	Treatment 2: America doesn't have much to fear from terrorists in coming years	23.5%	76.5%
Climate	**Treatment 1:** America will face more pressing concerns than climate change in the future	77.6%	22.4%
	Treatment 2: Climate change will seriously threaten our well-being in the future	74.7%	25.3%
Military	**Treatment 1:** America's comparative military strength will decline in the future	51.0%	49.0%
	Treatment 2: America will have most powerful military in the future	83.0%	17.0%
National Debt	**Treatment 1:** The debt will be a severe burden on today's children	86.7%	13.3%
	Treatment 2: The debt does not threaten the future economy	36.9%	63.1%

ences in the present. Each set of respondents, along with the control group that had not received a future forecast, was asked about its current policy preferences on the eight issues noted above. The results are quite striking. When asked, for example, whether the U.S. should prioritize economic growth or climate change, respondents answered in a manner consistent with their answer to the first question. Those who had been told that climate change was not a future threat and agreed favored policies emphasizing growth (68%); while those who had been told that climate change threatened our future well-being (and agreed) subsequently favored policies that made climate change a top priority (62%). The control group was much more closely divided (55% and 45%, respectively). Depending upon what future forecast they received, the two treatment groups expressed preferences that differ substantially from one another and from the control group. Table 3.2 displays this phenomenon for all policy areas. It would seem that alternative forecasts of the future can change respondents' preferences in the present.

TABLE 3.2. Manipulating the Future to Affect Present-Day Policy Preferences

Future Treatment	Present-Day Policy Preference (%)	
Immigration	Restrict immigration	Encourage immigration
Treatment 1: Agree immigration restrictions will make U.S. better	75.2	
Control	61.9	
Treatment 2: Agree immigration restrictions will make U.S. worse		73.1
Control		38.1
National Security	Invest in military	More work with international organizations
Treatment 1: Agree U.S. will be safer with more military strength	41.5	
Control	26.1	
Treatment 2: Agree U.S. will be safer with more international cooperation		77.0
Control		74.0
Economy	Leave economy to the private sector	Regulate economy more
Treatment 1: Agree it's better to reduce economic regulations in the future	67.5	
Control	39.5	

Treatment 2: Agree it's better to increase economic regulations in the future		60.4
Control		60.5

Foreign Policy	Improve relations with Russia	Improve relations with China
Treatment 1: Agree greatest threat will come from China	45.5	
Control	35.8	
Treatment 2: Agree greatest threat will come from Russia		73.1
Control		64.2

Terrorism	Strike terrorists first	Use diplomacy to solve problems
Treatment 1: Agree that it's likely terrorists will attack	50.9	
Control	48.8	
Treatment 2: Agree that there's not much to fear from terrorism		65.7
Control		51.2

Climate Change	Prioritize economy over climate change	Make climate change a top priority
Treatment 1: Agree U.S. will face more pressing concerns than climate change	67.6	
Control	54.7	
Treatment 2: Agree climate change seriously threatens our future		62.1
Control		45.3

Military	Prioritize military spending	Spend more on domestic issues
Treatment 1: Agree U.S. military strength will decline in the future	42.1	
Control	36.7	
Treatment 2: Agree U.S. will continue to have most powerful military		63.6
Control		63.3

National Debt	Cut entitlement programs	Maintain spending levels
Treatment 1: Agree debt will be severe burden in the future	53.0	
Control	47.6	
Treatment 2: Agree debt does not threaten future economy		67.0
Control		52.4

On average, as shown by figure 3.2, the policy preferences of those who receive a forecast of the future is changed 11.6 percentage points relative to untreated control groups. This change is somewhat less than the impact of the "history lessons" reviewed in the previous chapter, but it is still substantial and seems to indicate the powerful impact of revising forecasts of the future upon individuals' current preferences.

If we look more closely at the effects of a "history lesson" versus a future forecast on respondents' current policy preferences regarding identical pairs of issues (see figure 3.3), we see that history appears to have a greater effect than future forecasts on a majority of policy preferences.

This result may seem peculiar. After all, a forecast of rain should have a greater effect upon my decision to carry an umbrella than a history of rain in the region. Yet, as economists have noted, individuals tend to discount the future, seeing it as probabilistic and acting according to their interpretation of its present value. In the case of climate change, for example, most climate scientists are convinced that we must act now to avert disastrous consequences sometime in the future. The question, however, of how much to spend now to avoid problems in the distant future is subject to what is sometimes called a social discount rate, with most individuals (and governments) willing to spend only a few pennies now even if they accept warnings of dire consequences several centuries hence. The past, on the other hand, is not subject to such discounting. If individuals are convinced that an event took place, then it is a fact rather than a probability and is likely to have an undiscounted impact upon their current preferences.

The Dissidents

For each treatment group, despite the effects of acquiescence bias, a significant percentage of respondents expressed disagreement with the future forecast that constituted their group's "treatment." Among these dissidents an extremely high percentage subsequently expressed policy preferences inconsistent with the forecast they were given (see table 3.3). For example, those prompted to agree with the idea that the U.S. would be safer if it increased its military strength who, instead, disagreed were the strongest of all groups in their support for more emphasis on international cooperation. Similarly, those who disagreed with the assertion that climate change posed a future threat were the strongest of all groups in their support for prioritizing other problems relative to climate change.

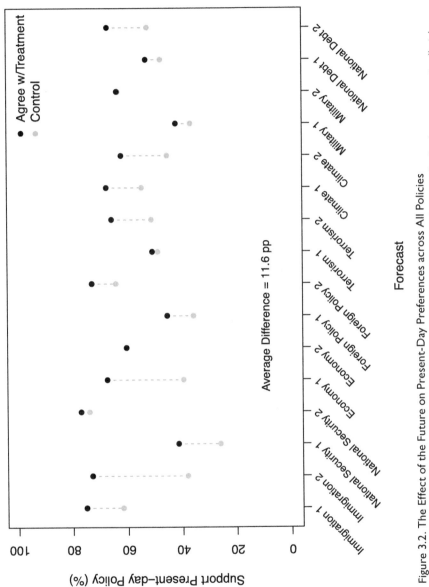

Figure 3.2. The Effect of the Future on Present-Day Preferences across All Policies
This figure visualizes the effect of future forecasts on present-day policy preferences for both treatments in all eight
policy areas.

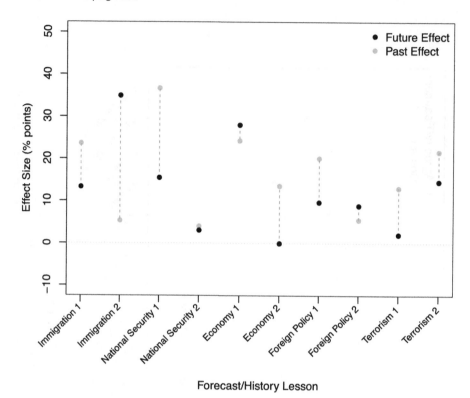

Figure 3.3. Comparison of Future and Past Effects on Present-Day Preferences
This figure shows that the effect of the past tends to be larger than the effect of the future on present-day policy preferences.

These dissidents, roughly 30 percent of all respondents, are individuals who support particular future narratives and react vigorously against attempts to introduce some alternative forecast. We see this in such cases as the furious attacks sometimes launched by climate scientists against those who question the prevalent model of climate change. One climate scientist recently declared that "climate change denial should be a crime," one that should be punished as severely as murder.[24]

Explaining Dissent

Who are the dissidents? Are they well-educated individuals who dismiss efforts to recast the future? An investigation of which factors drive dis-

TABLE 3.3. The Dissenters (Future Forecasts)

Policy Area (1)	Treatments (2)	% Disagreed with treatment (3)	Among those who disagreed, % who support a policy inconsistent with treatment (4)	% in Control group who support the same policy as those in Column 4 (5)
Immigration	**Treatment 1:** Immigration restrictions will make America better	24.8%	69.9%	38.1%
	Treatment 2: Immigration restrictions will make America worse	32.4%	86.2%	61.9%
War & Peace	**Treatment 1:** U.S. will be safer if it increases military strength in future	30.9%	94.0%	74.0%
	Treatment 2: U.S. will be safer with more international cooperation in future	13.3%	51.9%	26.1%
Economy	**Treatment 1:** Nations whose governments reduce regulations will be better off	38.4%	81.4%	60.5%
	Treatment 2: Nations whose governments increase regulations will be better off	5.0%	46.7%	39.5%
Foreign Policy	**Treatment 1:** Greatest threat to America will come from China in the future	43.6%	70.8%	64.2%
	Treatment 2: Greatest threat to America will come from Russia in the future	48.3%	47.9%	35.8%
Terrorism	**Treatment 1:** Likely terrorists will attack America in next decade	9.9%	63.8%	51.2%
	Treatment 2: America doesn't have much to fear from terrorists in coming years	76.5%	45.2%	48.8%
Climate	**Treatment 1:** America will face more pressing concerns than climate change in the future	22.4%	72.5%	45.3%
	Treatment 2: Climate change will seriously threaten our well-being in the future	25.3%	91.2%	54.7%
Military	**Treatment 1:** America's comparative military strength will decline in the future	49.0%	66.3%	63.3%
	Treatment 2: America will continue to have most powerful military in the future	17.1%	28.6%	36.7%
National Debt	**Treatment 1:** The debt will be a severe burden on today's children	13.3%	74.4%	52.4%
	Treatment 2: The debt does not threaten the future economy	63.1%	51.0%	47.6%

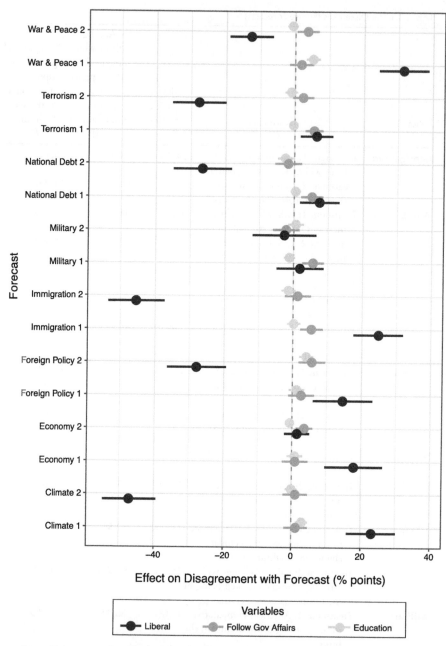

Figure 3.4. Explaining Dissent with Future Forecasts
This graph compares the effect of ideology, education, and political engagement (measured as the extent to which respondents follow government affairs) on their likelihood of disagreeing with the future forecast presented to them. The results show that the effect of ideology is strongest across nearly all policy areas.

sent reveals that political ideology, above all else, is the most influential. Figure 3.4 compares the effect of ideology, education, and political engagement on respondents' likelihood of disagreeing with the future forecast presented to them.[25] As is evident in the figure, the effect of ideology far exceeds the effect of education and political engagement (two well-documented determinants of political opinion). Note that the graph plots the effect of self-defining oneself as a liberal or strong liberal; the effects of self-defining oneself as a conservative or strong conservative would have the same strength but in the opposite direction. It seems that efforts to recast the future are most likely to be rejected by those whose credenda—not knowledge—cause them to reject new ideas. These ideologues, in fact, react negatively to efforts to teach them new versions of events and rush to affirm their support for policies inconsistent with the views of the future now being foisted upon them.

Forecasting the Future

Forecasting the future is always an uncertain business. Since it has not yet occurred, the future cannot be known. It can, nevertheless, be imagined and predicted. Imaginings and predictions of the future can have a significant impact upon the present as societies inquire into, plan for, and seek to reshape the future. Unlike the plots of science fiction tales, material objects from the future may not be able to appear in the present. Yet ideas from and about the future can materialize in the present where they affect conduct and, perhaps, change what might have been the future.

Since the future has not yet arrived, forecasts can be greeted with skepticism, especially by those with a stake in some other future. And, even if a forecast is convincing, willingness to act on the forecast may be subject to social discounting. Why take action on the climate today when the problems may not be fully manifest for many years? Nevertheless, forecasts about the future, like revision of the past, do have an impact upon policy preferences in the present.

Now, let us turn to the even more complex question of the relationship between the future and the past and how the two, together, can influence the present.

CHAPTER 4

How the Future Affects the Past

The future not only has an impact upon the present but it can also affect the past. Individuals, groups, and forces with a vision of the future will often seek to identify elements in the past that seem to presage or validate their future aspirations. As we saw in chapter 1, this effort can require some reinvention of the past to correspond to some idea of the future. If, moreover, this revised past is sufficiently compelling, groups in the present may seek to re-create it, in this way helping to bring about the imagined future. Thus, for example, proponents of an enlarged and more assertive role for Japan in the future frequently reimagine the Japanese past and point to examples of heroism and glory while ignoring or glossing over Japanese conduct in Korea and China before and during World War II. These same neonationalists attempt to revise the history of Japan's ill-advised decision to attack the United States and, instead, portray Japan as the victim rather than the instigator of armed conflict.[1] As this example suggests, moreover, the future and past can be reimagined combinatorially—essentially yoked together to bring added pressure upon present-day realities.

One important example of such an effort is what historian Jeffrey Olick has called "the politics of victimization and regret."[2] Through temporal reengineering, a vision of the future is linked to and powered by a recitation or reinvention of past grievances that can be used to justify even vicious and brutal action to achieve the desired present. Take, for example, the violence of the Balkan wars of the 1990s, which involved "ethnic cleansing" and the brutal murder of many thousands of civilians. In the former Yugoslavia, several ethnic groups including Serbs, Croats, Bosnian Muslims, and others harbored rival visions of future nationhood that led to conflicts after the collapse of the central government. What made these confrontations so brutal, though, as historian Ilana R. Bet-El observes, were the histories of grievance often invented by competing political elites to mobilize popular support for their various claims. The words "I remember," writes Bet-El, became "weapons of war" designed to make members of other ethnic groups abhorrent and thus to justify the use of any and all means to defeat them and secure the future for one's own ethnic followers.[3] Serbs recalled victimization by the Croat Ustashe during World War II. Croats recalled violence directed at them by Serbian partisans in that same war. As each sought to build a state of its own after the collapse of Yugoslavia, ethnic conflict was inflamed by "radicalized memories."[4]

The most common vehicles in which the past is reimagined so as to promote some vision of the future are literature and cinema. As to cinema, films that purport to be explorations of history are often efforts to make some point about the present or future using historical materials. One familiar example is *The Crucible*, Arthur Miller's stage and screenplay, which was first performed in 1953. Purporting to be an account of the Salem witch trials of the seventeenth century, the play and film present a thinly veiled attack on the anti-Communist "witch hunts" of the 1950s. Since a number of Hollywood directors and screenwriters were accused of subversive activities in these investigations, they retaliated by writing films in which villainous historical characters engage in politically motivated witch hunts. In a 1953 biblical epic, *The Robe*, the Roman emperor Caligula is depicted as an evil fellow with strikingly similar speech patterns to those of Senator Joseph McCarthy. In the film, Christians are portrayed as victims of McCarthy-like persecutions as Caligula attempts to hunt down and purge the subversives he imagines to have spread through the Roman Empire. Similarly, *Ivanhoe*, a 1952 film based on Sir Walter Scott's nineteenth-century novel, features a witchcraft trial in which, for political reasons, an innocent character is convicted of witchcraft on the basis of falsified evidence. Both films were written by screenwriters who had been compelled to appear before hearings of the House Un-American Activities Committees where they had been accused of Communist tendencies.[5]

In these two examples, a version of the past is created to make a point about the present. Often enough, however, some set of past events is cinematically reimagined to make a point about the future. For example, in a number of Nazi-era German films, a reimagined German (usually Prussian) history is employed to show the all-but-certain future benefits of

German unity, strong leadership, decisive action, and popular obedience. These themes are emphasized in a number of films made during the 1930s about the career of Frederick the Great—the so-called Fredericus films—as well as studies of the lives of other important historical figures like Otto von Bismarck. The Fredericus films point to a period when strong leadership brought about a renewal of German greatness, presumably pointing to the German future under Hitler. In the 1940 film *Bismarck*, the Prussian chancellor's iron will and determination serve as models for the characteristics needed to bring about a glorious German future. Nazi-era films also found many lessons in the early nineteenth century when, at least as imagined, heroic German forces rose up against the Napoleonic occupation, expelled the French, and demonstrated that German bravery and fortitude would again, as they had once before, throw off the disabilities imposed upon Germany by its foreign foes.[6]

Germans hardly have a monopoly on this use of history to promote values deemed important for the future. Film historian Brian Taves has argued that what he calls American historical adventure films are metaphorical accounts that assert the "timeless need for liberty and freedom." The histories imagined in these films are actually stories meant to offer guidance to those living in the present to help them achieve some imagined future.[7]

Very often novels and films set in the past but speaking to the present and future attempt to depict some imagined past as a lost "golden age." The idea of the golden age represents a not-so-subtle rebuke to the present and not-at-all subtle beacon lighting the way to a better future. The term "Golden Age" derives from the ancient Greek notion of the four ages of man. For the Greeks, the Golden Age was a time of legend when humans were good, noble, pure, and prosperous and lived long lives in the company of the gods. The subsequent ages of man represent declines from this ideal world.

In American films, the golden age seems to be found in idyllic small towns in the first half of the twentieth century. These towns, like Grover's Corners in *Our Town* (1940), Bedford Falls in *It's a Wonderful Life* (1946), and Ithaca, California in *The Human Comedy* (1943), are depicted as friendly places where citizens are honest, hardworking, and overwhelmingly white. The characters encounter problems but face them with stiff upper lips and rely on pluck, determination, and individual self-help to succeed. Occasionally, characters find small town life unsatisfying but they learn to accept it, and, if they have left, they learn their lesson and return, as the title of one film, *Why Girls Go Back Home* (1926), indicates.

The America depicted in these films has no crime, no social problems, and no racial problems. This idyllic America is an implicit rebuke to the turbulent and sometimes violent reality of the present. Indeed, this rebuke is made explicitly in *Pleasantville* (1998). When the imaginary eponymous town, initially seen on the screen in black and white, begins to be shown in color, the result is turmoil. The new, more colorful community is livelier and intellectually interesting but lacks the commitment to communal values of the old Pleasantville. In all these films, the solution to America's problems seems clear. The nation must recapture the verities and virtues that once made America great—to return in the future to the values of the golden age of the past. Interestingly, while American golden age films point to a mythical past of social equality and individualism, German golden age films, particularly during the Nazi era, were likely to be set in the court of Frederick the Great and to focus on a golden age of leadership, service, and military valor.

Alternate History

Another literary and cinematic genre in which the past is reimagined to make some point about the future is "alternate history." This genre is often set in an imagined present or future resulting from a past that differed in important ways from the familiar past. Alternate histories written in the United States usually focus on the imagined consequences of a Nazi German victory in the Second World War or a Confederate victory in the American Civil War. In both cases, the reimagined history results in a bleak future and the general point seems to be to validate decisions made during each of these two critical periods. A well-known example of the Nazi victory alternate history is Robert Harris's best-selling 1992 novel (later presented as a television film), *Fatherland*.

Narrated by a character in the near future, the story is set in the reimagined 1960s and is premised on the idea that the Normandy invasion was a failure, forcing the United States to withdraw its troops from Europe though continuing to prosecute the war against Japan to a successful conclusion. After the American withdrawal, Germany invades and defeats England and consolidates its control over Western Europe, combining the conquered European nations into a single state named Germania. The Soviet Union has been largely defeated but not conquered and continues to fight a vicious guerrilla war against the Nazis. Though not officially at war with one another, what amounts to a "cold war" between the U.S. and Germania has continued since the end of actual hostilities. Between the cold war with the U.S. and the guerrilla war against the Russians, the Germanian economy is severely stressed and is slowly collapsing. As a result of its economic stagnation, Germania is anxious to improve relations with the U.S., and sees in the election of Joseph P. Kennedy, who had advocated American neutrality during the war, a chance to mend fences with the Americans. Unfortunately for this plan, a heroic reporter's public revelation of what had been kept secret—the German extermination of Europe's Jews—forces Kennedy to rebuff Germanian overtures and eventually leads to Germania's economic disintegration.

Fatherland and the various other alternate histories premised upon the idea of German victory in World War II, including such works as *The Man in the High Castle* and *It Happened Here*, share a number of common themes. First, they validate the present by pointing to the horrors of a future in which history took a different turn, particularly a turn that reduced the power of the United States of America. Without a powerful America various malign forces are able to work their will upon the world. This theme of the need for American power and leadership is also emphasized by future histories in which the Confederacy won the Civil War. These works, moreover, valorize particular character traits, most notably courage, needed to keep history and hence the future on the right track. Courageous leaders like Winston Churchill and Franklin Delano Roosevelt and brave ordinary individuals play critical roles. Looking back from the future in these works, we usually find that cowardice and irresolution in the past allowed evil persons and their ideas to seize control of the future. Finally, these works (at least those produced for American audiences) are generally paeans to liberal democracy. A future without liberal democracy is a bleak and harrowing place where individuals literally live in constant fear of the Gestapo.

Irredentism

Revision of the past to point to a desired future is a tactic often employed by irredentist movements. There is hardly a square inch of territory on the face of the earth that did not once belong to some group other than its current occupants. Most often, large-scale property transfers depended upon the use of force, with the victors writing a history papering over or justifying their conquest. The territory of the United States was forcibly taken from Native American tribes or seized from Spaniards who had previously stolen it from Native American tribes. This brutal history of land theft was largely ignored by American history texts or even celebrated as exemplifying America's divine mission or Manifest Destiny. In recent years, politically progressive Americans have begun to lament what they now regard as the injustice done to the Native Americans. This sympathy, however, seems too late in coming since few Native Americans have survived.

In other parts of the world, however, conquered and expropriated groups retain sufficient numbers and cultural identity to attempt to reclaim what they believe to be their rightful homelands. For such groups, historical evidence of their previous land ownership as well as evidence of perfidy by the current landholders is key to mobilizing support among their own compatriots and winning the sympathy of external audiences. Generally, such groups find it useful to retouch the past just a bit to make it comport as closely as possible with the desired future.

Take, for example, the case of Scottish nationalism. Scotland has, during some periods of its history, been an independent entity and during others has shared a monarch with England. In 1290, Edward I of England claimed overlordship of Scotland, touching off a series of wars that eventually placed the House of Stuart on the Scottish throne. After the death of Elizabeth I of England, the English throne was assumed by her nearest relative who happened to be the Stuart King James VI of Scotland. In this way, the House of Stuart gained control of the English throne, as well, and from 1603 to 1688, with an interregnum between 1653 and 1659, the Stuarts ruled both England and Scotland in what was called the Union of the Crowns. Stuart rule, however, came to an end in 1688 largely because of the religious struggles of the era.

The last Stuart king, James II, was a Catholic and thus not fully accepted by most of the English or Scottish nobility, which was by now heavily Protestant. James's daughter and heir-presumptive, Mary, was a Protestant so the nobility was content to wait for her to succeed to the throne. This reticence was ended when a Catholic son and new heir-apparent was born to James, promising a continuation of Catholic rule in the realm. For this and other reasons, James was deposed by the nobility in the so-called Glorious Revolution and followed on the throne by James's Protestant daughter,

Mary II, and her Protestant husband, James's nephew, William of Orange, who were, in turn succeeded by George I of the House of Hanover. During the rule of Mary and William, England and Scotland were formally united under the Treaty of Union of 1707, replacing the Union of the Crowns with the United Kingdom.

These events led to a rebellion in parts of Scotland known as the Jacobite movement, which persisted for some 50 years. The Jacobites, whose chief base of support was a number of Highland clans, hoped to restore the Stuart monarchy in England and Scotland or, failing that, to gain the independence of Scotland under a Stuart king. In the 1740s, the Jacobites supported a rebellion designed to win the Scottish throne for Charles Edward Stuart, known as "Bonnie Prince Charlie." Despite several military successes, Prince Charlie was defeated and forced into exile in France and Italy, effectively ending the rebellion.

The idea of Scottish independence seemed to end with the defeat of the Jacobites. For the next 200 years, Scots were among the driving forces of British imperial expansion and Scottish regiments were the mainstays of the British army. Few voices in Scotland favored a break with England, though the question of greater home rule for Scotland was sometimes debated. The decline of the British Empire after World War II opened the way for a resurgence of nationalist sentiment and the rise of a nationalist movement in Scotland as union with England no longer seemed to give Scotland a share of world leadership. The discovery of oil off the Scottish coast in 1970 introduced the idea that Scotland might be economically better off on its own. "It's our oil" became a nationalist slogan. These matters came to a head in the devolution referendum of 1997 and the independence referendum of 2014. The former resulted in the creation of a Scottish parliament and a greater measure of home rule in Scotland. The latter, sponsored by the Scottish National Party, might have resulted in the dissolution of the union with England and complete Scottish independence. The referendum failed, but the idea of independence continues to have substantial support in Scotland.

To bolster support for the idea of a free and independent Scotland, leaders of the Scottish National Party have rewritten the Scottish past to comport with their vision of the Scottish future. The Scottish past, according to independence advocates, was one in which a free and independent nation was first bullied and then conquered by a neighboring power even though Scots like William Wallace (depicted in the popular film *Bravehe-*

art) fought resolutely for Scottish freedom. This power, England, for centuries deprived Scots of control over their own affairs and suppressed their language and culture. As one author put it, the Scottish nationalist story "is essentially the narrative of an intrinsically antagonistic relationship in which a small but proud nation is pitted against a far greater power, both in terms of population and resources. It tells of how England has posed a persistent threat to the survival and success of the Scottish nation through constant meddling and attempts to impose its will on the people of Scotland. It is also a question of bullying and treachery, whereby a range of events can be highlighted as evidence that the English cannot be trusted."[8]

Leaving aside the question of whether medieval Scotland was actually a nation, rather than a congeries of clans and fiefdoms, one might wonder if the Scottish nationalist view is much more than a historical stretch prompted by a small group of politicians seeking to create a state they might govern. Perhaps England's Tudor kings were aggressive in seeking to expand their domains, but they were succeeded by the Scottish House of Stuart that ruled England for nearly a century. Subsequently, Scots dominated the British army and Britain's colonial governments. In modern times, more than a dozen of Britain's prime ministers were of Scottish extraction and one of Britain's two major political parties, the Labour Party, was founded and frequently led by Scottish politicians. Perhaps the English should feel aggrieved at centuries of Scottish domination. But, whether accurate or not, Scottish separatist politicians have found it useful to rewrite history to comport with a hoped-for future. And, according to poll data, a sizeable number of Scotland's residents seem persuaded by the nationalist's revisionist account, with an overwhelming majority of Scotland's residents identifying themselves as Scottish rather than British when asked to choose.[9] And, of course, only a slight majority voted to keep Scotland in the United Kingdom in the 2014 national referendum.

There are, of course, many other examples of nationalist and irredentist movements employing historical revisionism to bring the past into alignment with an imagined future. One is the contemporary Catalan independence movement, which seeks to bring about the secession of Catalonia from Spain. This movement has developed an elaborate if sometimes fanciful Catalan history that includes the celebration of September 11 as the Catalan national holiday, commemorating the date in 1714 when Catalan independence was allegedly extinguished by Spanish aggression during the so-called War of the Spanish Succession.

Most historians view this war as a dynastic rather than a national struggle, involving as it did complicated dynastic claims that affected Europe's major royal houses. To protect their privileges, much of the Catalan nobility fought on the side of the Habsburg dynasty's claim to the Spanish throne. The Habsburgs were defeated, resistance ending on September 11, 1714, and the Bourbon, Philip V, brought all of Spain, including Catalonia, under his control. The Catalan nobility lost some of the special privileges it had enjoyed under the Habsburgs, but Catalonia had no more been an independent entity under Habsburg rule than it became under the Bourbons. Over the next century, however, numerous historical works were published in the Catalan language lamenting these events and purporting to demonstrate Catalonia's unique character, hence giving "meaning and legitimacy" to the creation of a future Catalonian state.[10] In the Catalan case, preservation of the region's historic language proved to be a major portal to an alternative history. Spain's central government, unlike, say, its French neighbor, failed to suppress regional dialects and so left open a useful vehicle for irredentist movements.

Zionism and Palestinian Nationalism

Competing historical revisionisms help to fuel the ongoing dispute between Israelis and Palestinians over the proper ownership of the land of Israel. Israelis base their claims upon the Hebrew Bible and upon a historical account associated with the Zionist movement. In the Hebrew Bible, of course, God promises Abraham that he will give his descendants as a perpetual possession, "all the land from the river of Egypt to the Euphrates" (Genesis 15:18–21). This land came to be called the Promised Land or the Land of Israel. Hebrews or Israelites, later called *yehudim* or Jews, occupied some or all of this land from, perhaps, 2000 B.C. until an unsuccessful revolt against the Romans led Roman authorities in 70 A.D. to expel all but a handful of the survivors to other parts of the empire. Even then, religious prophecy declared that the Jews would return. According to the Prophet Isaiah:

> And in that day there shall be a root of Jesse, which shall stand for
> an ensign of the people; to it shall the Gentiles seek: and his rest
> shall be glorious. And it shall come to pass in that day, that the Lord

shall set his hand again the second time to recover the remnant of his people, which shall be left, from Assyria, and from Egypt, and from Pathros, and from Cush, and from Elam, and from Shinar, and from Hamath, and from the islands of the sea. And he shall set up an ensign for the nations, and shall assemble the outcasts of Israel, and gather together the dispersed of Judah from the four corners of the earth. (Isaiah 11:10–12)

Religious Jews and most evangelical Protestants regard this biblical promise and prophecy to be decisive affirmations of Jewish claims to the land of Israel. The Zionist movement, for its part, developed a more secular history to promote Jewish claims to the Promised Land. Zionism is a secular, nationalist ideology developed in response to the persecution of Jews in Europe. After considering and rejecting other possible homelands including such seemingly implausible possibilities as Uganda, European Zionists focused on the historic ties of Jews to the land of Israel as the legitimating basis for the return of the Jews to their ancestral homeland and the future re-creation of a State of Israel. This Zionist perspective is affirmed in Israel's Declaration of Independence:

The Land of Israel was the birthplace of the Jewish people. Here their spiritual, religious and political identity was shaped. Here they first attained to statehood, created cultural values of national and universal significance and gave to the world the eternal Book of Books.

After being forcibly exiled from their land, the people kept faith with it throughout their Dispersion and never ceased to pray and hope for their return to it and for the restoration in it of their political freedom. Impelled by this historic and traditional attachment, Jews strove in every successive generation to re-establish themselves in their ancient homeland. In recent decades they returned in masses.

Before World War II, much of the ancient Promised Land lay within a territory known as Palestine, which, for several centuries, had been a province of Ottoman Turkey. In 1920, upon the collapse of the Ottoman Empire, Palestine came to be governed by Britain under a League of Nations mandate. During the interwar period, several tens of thousands of European Jews migrated to Palestine where they joined small Jewish communities that had been established during the Ottoman period. By the time of the war some 500,000 Jews lived under British rule in Palestine. More might have emigrated to Palestine but the British thought that large-scale Jewish immigration would cause unrest among the Arabs and so limited immigration to a trickle.

After World War II, half a million Jewish survivors were housed in displaced persons camps in occupied Germany. These refugees could not return to their former homes in Eastern Europe and were not welcome in the United States or Western Europe. At the same time, Jewish communities in Palestine were demanding the creation of an independent Jewish state and engaged in a small-scale guerrilla war against the British to press their claims. The U.S. saw the creation of a Jewish state in Palestine as a logical solution for the refugee problem and, ignoring British misgivings, secured a United Nations vote in 1948 partitioning Palestine into separate Jewish and Arab states. Palestinian Arabs, supported by the armies of several Arab states, refused to accept the UN resolution and launched a military effort to prevent the creation of a Jewish state. This Arab effort was a disastrous failure and allowed Jewish military forces to expand the territory of the newly declared State of Israel beyond those mandated by the United Nations. During, and in the aftermath of, the 1948 war, more than 700,000 Arabs left their homes in Palestine, many settling in refugee camps then located in Jordan and Egypt where many of their descendants remain though the sites are now Gaza and the West Bank.

As in the cases of Scottish and Catalonian nationalists, Zionists developed a historical narrative that bolstered their claims to the establishment of a state of Israel. According to the Zionist narrative, Jews continued to live in the land of Israel after the Romans expelled them in 70 A.D., maintaining a continuing physical attachment to the land. In modern times, as more Jews arrived, they purchased land from the Arabs, never seeking to forcibly dispossess them. Even during and after the 1948 war, this narrative holds, Jews made every effort to avoid a mass Arab exodus. Zionists also resurrected the Hebrew language, which virtually no nineteenth- or twentieth-century Jews spoke, to underscore the alleged continuity between the Jewish future and the Hebrew past.

The Zionist historical account, of course, glosses over the fact that after 70 A.D., for more than a thousand years, few if any Jews resided in the Holy Land. Jews continued to have a religious attachment to the land of

Israel but, for secular Zionists, the strength of this attachment was apparently not so great since some were willing to consider establishing a Jewish homeland elsewhere. And, as to the idea that Arabs left the new State of Israel voluntarily after the 1948 war, few contemporary Israeli historians would make this claim. As is so often the case, groups defeated in a war were forced to cede territory and relocate, as happened again after the 1967 war.

For their part, the descendants of the former Arab inhabitants of what is now the State of Israel, calling themselves Palestinians, have developed a counternarrative designed to support their hope of displacing the Jews and replacing Israel with a Palestinian state. According to this Palestinian narrative, the Palestinian people have possessed a national identity for several centuries and had begun to form a proto state prior to the creation of the State of Israel. The establishment of Israel and its military victory, known to Palestinians as the Nakba, or the catastrophe of 1948, represented an illegitimate land seizure by foreign Jews, supported by Western powers. These selfsame Jews again employed force to expand their territories in 1967, displacing or persecuting the legitimate Palestinian owners of the land. This series of aggressive and illegal land thefts can only be countered by force, leading to the re-creation of a Palestinian state stretching from the Jordan River to the Mediterranean Sea.

This narrative, like the others we have discussed, attempts to reinvent the past to coincide with a hoped-for future. The idea of Palestinians as a self-conscious national group is quite recent. Until it fell under British rule in 1920, Palestine was simply another Ottoman province inhabited by Arabs with no particular local identity. Palestinian nationalism developed largely in response to Zionism.[11] In a sense, Palestinian national identity and the idea of a Palestinian state were as much results of Zionism as the State of Israel. As to the aggressive and perfidious conduct of the Jews, the 1948 war, the 1967 war, and, later, the 1973 war were products of Arab attacks on Israel so, at least by that measure, the aggressiveness of the Israelis is at least matched by that of the Arabs.

As in the case of the Balkans, noted above, rival national aspirations are inflamed by imagined histories and senses of past grievance on the part of both Israelis and Palestinians. Recent surveys published by the Palestinian Center for Policy and Survey Research, as well as surveys by Israeli academics, point to the fact that Palestinians' understanding of history, and the sense of grievance imbedded in the historical narrative that is most widely shared among Palestinians, promote and legitimate violence. Thus, nearly three-fourths of Palestinian respondents to one survey denied that Jews had a long history in Jerusalem while more than 90 percent thought Palestinians had such a history. More than 90 percent of Palestinians surveyed believe that Israel does not abide by the terms of its agreements. Most Palestinians believe Israel guilty of having implemented "diabolical" plans to drive Palestinians out of Jerusalem and to destroy Islamic holy places there. This historical narrative, in turn, justifies campaigns of shootings, bombings, and knifings aimed at Israeli civilians. Indeed, most Palestinians surveyed said they did not regard such actions as terrorism, but merely as forms of self-defense justified by Israel's past history. In this way, the words "I remember" become weapons of war designed to build a future from the rubble of the past.[12]

Acceptance of the Palestinian historical narrative by various European and American progressives has fueled a movement calling for the boycott of Israeli products, divestment by governments and corporations from Israeli companies, and international sanctions against Israel. Thus, we have another instance in which a history imagined to comport with a desired future stimulates political action in the present.

The Future and the Past

In chapters 2 and 3, we were able to show that changing respondents' perceptions of the past or future could affect their policy preferences in the present. As we saw above, however, a number of governments and political forces have sought to cumulate revisions of the past and future, rewriting the past to comport with some imagined future and yoking the two together to smash established realities.

Based upon the empirical evidence we present below, this political tactic seems to have considerable power. First, a vision of the future can be used to affect respondents' ideas about the past. Second, if successfully brought into alignment, conceptions of the past and future, together, can exert a more powerful impact upon current policy preferences than either alone.

To demonstrate the first idea, respondents were randomly assigned to treatment and control groups. Members of the treatment group were further divided into two subgroups and given competing forecasts of future events. For example, members of Subgroup A were told that immigration restrictions would enhance America's future while those assigned to Subgroup B were told that restricting immigration would leave America worse off in the future.

Subsequently, the members of each subgroup who agreed with the prediction they were given (about 65%) were presented with a series of assertions about the past designed to correspond by subject matter to the future forecasts they had received. Respondents assigned to the control group that was not given a forecast of the future were presented with the same historical assertions. We then compared the responses of the treatment groups and the control group to the ten assertions about history presented to them. Table 4.1 reports the results.

As we saw in chapter 3, individuals will generally agree with forecasts of the future presented to them. Our current results suggest that those who receive and accept a particular forecast of the future are subsequently more likely to see the past through the same lens. Take, for example, the question of immigration restrictions. Among those who agreed with a forecast suggesting that immigration restrictions would have future benefits, 72.3 percent subsequently agreed with the assertion that immigration had historically been a bad thing. Among members of the control group, that is, the group not exposed to a future forecast, only 56.3 percent agreed with the historical assertion.

Similarly, among those who agreed with a forecast suggesting that immigration restrictions would have negative future consequences, 47.3 percent then agreed with the assertion that immigration had historically been a bad thing—an assertion with which only 34.5 percent of the control group members agreed. It would appear that securing respondents' agreement with predictions of the future can alter at least some individuals' understandings of the past, bringing those respondents' conceptions of the past and future into conformity.

The creation of conformity between past and future views, in turn, has substantial implications for the present, more successfully altering present-day preferences than changing past or future perspectives alone. To illustrate this point, we presented respondents with pairs of assertions about contemporary topics. Each pair of assertions presented the same perspective couched in two different ways—as a history lesson and as a future forecast. Thus, for example, some respondents were told that, historically, immigration had been bad for America and that, in the future, immigra-

TABLE 4.1. The Effect of the Future on the Past

Policy Area	Forecast (treatment)	Treatment Group Among those who agreed with forecast, % who support corresponding history lesson	Control Group Among those not given a forecast, % who support history lesson
Immigration	**Forecast 1:** Immigration restrictions will make America better	72.3%	56.3%
	Forecast 2: Immigration restrictions will make America worse	47.3%	34.5%
War and Peace	**Forecast 1:** U.S. will be safer if it increases military strength in future	96.2%	76.9%
	Forecast 2: U.S. will be safer with more international cooperation in future	73.4%	74.3%
Economy	**Forecast 1:** Nations whose governments reduce regulations will be better off	87.6%	66.8%
	Forecast 2: Nations whose governments increase regulations will be better off	60.6%	56.3%
Foreign Policy	**Forecast 1:** Greatest threat to America will come from China in the future	40.6%	44.2%
	Forecast 2: Greatest threat to America will come from Russia in the future	70.5%	64.6%
Terrorism	**Forecast 1:** Likely terrorists will attack America in next decade	76.3%	71.6%
	Forecast 2: America doesn't have much to fear from terrorists in coming years	87.5%	65.5%

tion would hurt America. Other respondents were told that, historically, immigration had been good for America and that, in the future, immigration would help America. All respondents were then asked their current policy preferences on the matter in question. For example, on the issue of immigration, respondents were asked whether they currently favored restricting or easing entry into the U.S. A second group of respondents was given only a future prediction or a history lesson and asked whether they agreed or disagreed. Figure 4.1 reports the results.

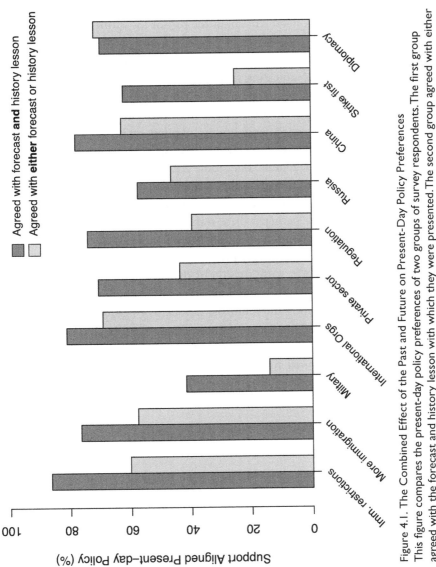

Figure 4.1. The Combined Effect of the Past and Future on Present-Day Policy Preferences

This figure compares the present-day policy preferences of two groups of survey respondents. The first group agreed with the forecast and history lesson with which they were presented. The second group agreed with either the forecast or the history lesson (meaning they disagreed with one of these). The figure shows that those who agree with consistent assertions about the past and present are more likely to express congruent, present-day policy preferences.

It seems quite apparent that those who agree with consistent assertions about the past and the future are far more likely to express current policy preferences congruent with those assertions than those who are offered and agree with only with a statement about the past **or** the future (respondents who receive inconsistent prompts are discussed in the next chapter). Take, for example, respondents who say they agree with both prospective and retrospective accounts indicating that America is more secure when it acts aggressively against its potential enemies. More than 60 percent of these respondents agree that America should strike first when confronted by foreign foes. On the other hand, among respondents who are presented with and agree only with prospective or retrospective accounts supporting aggressive military actions, only some 25 percent agree that America should strike first when threatened by foreign foes. It seems that imagining the past and predicting the future can have a cumulative impact.

On the one hand, perhaps, these results might not seem surprising. Two "treatments" have a more powerful effect than one. What of it? Recall, however, that this seemingly unsurprising fact has substantial political significance. Political forces with a vision of the future will often endeavor to invent a past consistent with that vision to mobilize and energize their followers. Hidden among the mundane numbers of figure 4.1 are shades of the *Dolchstoss*, the Lost Cause, Bonnie Prince Charlie, and a host of other pasts designed to bolster support, and, indeed, foment violence, on behalf of some imagined future. Thus, our rather innocuous-appearing figure offers an important political lesson. Those able to bring the past into conformity with the future can exercise considerable power.

Conclusion

The Uncertainty of Reality

In the political realm, time is not unilinear. The past, even when literally carved in stone, is subject to erosion, revision, and erasure. The 1,700-year-old stone statues of Buddha destroyed by the Taliban, the antiquities wrecked by ISIS in Iraq and Syria, the gradual disappearance of America's Confederate monuments, and the colonial-era monuments and statues smashed and removed from their pedestals throughout Africa all show how fleeting even history carved in stone can be.[1] In all these cases groups currently wielding power sought to erase the memory of a history now inconsistent with their views and visions of the future. And, just as the past can be reshaped by political action in the present, the events of the present are often responses to future expectations that are, themselves, subject to present-day manipulation. In our simple experiments, "history lessons" could move contemporary policy preferences by an average of 16 percentage points; forecasts of the future could move contemporary policy preferences by an average of 12 percentage points; and the two together an average of 21 percentage points. And, to give the entire matter an Orwellian flavor, in the case of history lessons, we estimate an average "erasure effect" of 8.5 percentage points—the difference between those with long-held preferences and those whose preferences had been changed but seemed not to recall that they previously held other preferences.

Science fiction plots notwithstanding, physical objects cannot be sent from the future to alter the present or from the present to change the past. Ideas, though, <u>can</u> be sent on such journeys, and, even if they lack materiality at the start, ideas can materialize when they reach their new temporal destination. The future can be reimagined in order to change beliefs and conduct in the present. The past may be reinvented to affect behavior in the present and future. As we observed earlier, this materialization of temporally excursive ideas seems to exemplify the notion that reality is subject to the influence of consciousness.

Three propositions follow from these observations. First, the fact that the past, present, and future are subject to human manipulation suggests that history is driven by ideas and is not simply the product of impersonal forces, material conditions, or past choices. Humans are the architects of history, not its captives. Second, what we conceive to be political reality is rather tenuous. Changes in our understanding of the past or future can quite substantially alter general perceptions of and action in the present. Third, manipulation of time, especially the relationship between past and future, can function as a powerful political tool. In essence, political reality can be politically determined. Past, present, and future are not givens. They are products of political struggle, and victories in those struggles are, in turn, subject to future revision as emergent political forces find that the currently accepted past and future are inconsistent with their own ideas and interests. Let us examine each of these notions in turn.

Ideas and History

As we have observed, ideas about the future can change conceptions of the past and produce material changes in the present. New beliefs in the present can lead to efforts to revise the story of the past, which can, in turn, produce behavioral changes in the present. The power of ideas to travel in time and produce material change along nonlinear paths raises questions about several historical perspectives in the social sciences. Let us consider, in particular, historicism and the question of materialist versus idealist accounts of history.

We take the central idea of historicism in its various forms to be that history develops inexorably, according to discoverable principles and rules, toward some particular end. Some historicists, like Oswald Spengler, Arnold Toynbee, and, more recently, Samuel Huntington, claimed to have identified periods or stages through which civilizations pass. Most see history as largely the product of impersonal economic, social, or even biological forces such as epidemics, and tend to discount human agency as a causal factor.

Our observations, which are generally supportive of Karl Popper's famous critique of historicism, suggest that history lacks directionality and can—and often is—revised and rewritten to more fully comport with present-day perspectives and future aspirations. In the revision of history, human agency is paramount. Political and social forces create and re-create history according to their own purposes and goals.[2] Thus, as we have seen, the history of Southern White heroism during the American Civil War and White suffering after the war has been superseded by a history of White cupidity and Black fortitude. Even the statues and other artifacts attesting to the previous history are being removed from public spaces so as not to validate the former account. On the other hand, Scottish nationalists and Catalonian separatists, both losers in past struggles, have launched vigorous campaigns to revise history in order to reverse the outcomes of long-ago conflicts. In both cases, history is contingent, unsettled, lacking in any particular directionality, and subject to human agency. This idea is the temporal analog to the idea of constructivism in international relations theory, which sees most aspects of the international system as social constructs rather than given by nature.[3]

Of the several historicist schools of thought, historical institutionalism deserves particular mention. Historical institutionalism, popular among political scientists, is the least deterministic of the historicist perspectives. The central idea of historical institutionalism is path dependence, which means that taking any particular political or social path, while it does not predetermine the future, does pave the way for other future choices while foreclosing alternative possibilities.

This conception of path dependence seems plausible, but the historical image it presents is one of a road with occasional forks where choices are made that lead in some directions and away from others. Consider, though, a more complicated world represented by a tangle of paths through a dark forest. Rather than forking neatly, they may wind around, criss-cross, and backtrack. Contending political forces might seek to erase all memory of previous paths to prevent turnabouts, or to create memories of earlier paths and choices that had not previously existed, in order to facilitate critical reexamination of imagined forks in the historical road. Thus, at least as currently specified, historical institutionalism seems overly restrictive of human agency.

Idealism and Materialism

It, perhaps, follows from the foregoing discussion that in the debate between idealist and materialist conceptions of historical change, we come down on the side of idealism. Leaving aside quantum theorists' doubts about the reality of matter, we can certainly admit that material conditions and, of course, objects can have a powerful impact on history.[4] History before the existence of humans, for example, was greatly affected by meteor strikes on the planet and human history by such material things as volcanoes, plagues, and floods. Matter has a certain vibrancy, to use the terminology favored by political philosopher Jane Bennett.[5]

As we saw, however, history is also the product of ideas and consciousness and its material expressions are subject to revision. In response to expectations about the future and beliefs about the past, groups and individuals may set about changing the material world in substantial ways, building massive systems of levees to prevent floods, developing vaccines against plagues, and even planning space defenses against meteorites. In response to ideational changes in the present, even material history is subject to revision and erasure as the previously noted removal of Confederate monuments in America and pre-Islamic artifacts in Afghanistan attests.

Material objects do, to be sure, have a certain tenacity. Floods, plagues, and meteors may break through ingenuously constructed defenses. And, as to the revision of material history, it is not always easy to erase buildings and monuments, especially if these are vigorously defended by guardians of the old history. All these things, however, can be accomplished as history is rewritten and reshaped by groups whose vision of the future and present leads them to rewrite the past.

The Fragility of Political Reality

Political reality is fragile. Small ideational changes along one temporal dimension can produce large changes along others and even reverberate back to the original dimension in sometimes surprising ways. Reality is especially vulnerable to manipulation and alteration by measurement. The fragility of reality is exemplified by the phenomenon of acquiescence bias in surveys, which formed an important element of our study design. As we noted, most respondents are inclined to agree rather than disagree with an authoritative statement. Hence, in our study, when told that drops in crime rates were the product of "get tough" policies, 65 percent of the respondents in our national sample agreed. On the other hand, when told that better educational and social services were the chief reason crime declined between 1980 and 2010, 65 percent of respondents agreed that this was the right answer.[6]

Even though answers on the causes of drops in crime rates might seem dependent upon the way in which the question was asked rather than any deeply held belief, when asked a question about future policy—whether lawlessness was best curbed through stiff sentences or through social programs—respondents answered in a manner consistent with their answer to the first question. It seems that the process of measurement, in this case the manner in which the question was asked, had shaped reality for many respondents.

What seems to be true at a microscopic level is also true at a more macroscopic level. The process of measurement tugs and twists and warps reality, reshaping the present and future and, perhaps, the past as well. For example, as Benjamin Ginsberg has shown, public opinion polls do not simply measure, but produce changes in the character and identity of the views receiving public expression.[7] Opinion polls, moreover, as has been noted by Robert Weissberg, among others, generally ask respondents what they think the government should do about various economic, social, and international matters.[8] The problem, here, is that over time these questions create and bolster a state-centric reality in which the government is expected to do things. Alternate possibilities in which the government is not a key problem solver are generally ignored by surveys. In this way, measurement helps to nudge the future in one possible direction rather than others.

A similar point can be made about macroeconomic forecasting. Most, albeit perhaps not all, forecasting models are designed to determine which governmental economic policies are likely to be the best responses to future economic conditions. Measurement of future trends thus becomes a justification for one or another form of present-day government intervention into the economy, including the creation of new tools of government intervention, and the evolution of a more active role for the state.[9] In this way forecasting serves as a form of measurement that, whether by accident or design, shapes as much as it predicts the future.

Temporal Politics

These thoughts, in turn, suggest the power of what might be called *temporal politics* or *timing*. This is a form of political struggle in which contending political forces endeavor to revise the past to change the present and future or reimagine the future to change the present in a manner analogous to, though not identical with, such science fiction tales as *The Terminator*.

Three temporal strategies are especially noteworthy:

1. Reinvention of the past to affect the present. As we saw in chapter 2, as in Orwell's *1984*, contending political forces often seek to erase or rewrite the past in order to bolster their claims in the present. For centuries, Christians and Muslims destroyed ancient Egyptian artifacts. After the destruction of the Aztec and Inca Empires, the victorious Spaniards destroyed most of the defeated empires' most important religious and cultural symbols. At the conclusion of World War II, the victorious Allies systematically destroyed physical reminders of the defeated Nazi regime. And, as we have seen in recent years, radical Islamic groups such as the Taliban and ISIS have systematically destroyed ancient shrines and monuments throughout the Middle East in an effort to erase all vestiges of the region's pre-Islamic history. Even if these groups are militarily defeated in the present, their erasure of portions of the past may, by removing visible reminders of a prior history, reverberate through the region's future.

2. Imagination of a future to stimulate action in the present. As we saw in chapter 3, contending forces often seek to mobilize support in the present by pointing to a better future. Examples include the mundane world of electoral politics where such futuristic slogans as "change we can believe in" are commonplace. More important are teleological ideologies such as Marxism or Nazism or radical Islam pointing to a glorious future in whose name individuals are asked to sacrifice even their lives in the present.[10] And, as noted above, forecasting and measurement can become tools that point to a particular future requiring, in turn, some particular form of action in the present.

3. Reinvention of the past to comport with an imagined future. As we saw in chapter 4, this is among the most powerful tempo-

ral strategies and is often the driver of such ideologies as radical populism. This strategy that has been used quite effectively by irredentist movements such as the Scottish and Catalan nationalists who have invented histories of past humiliations at the hands of their lands' British and Spanish rulers, respectively. Accompanying the reinvented past is an imagined glorious future as an independent nation. The invented history of past grievances produces anger and the imagined glorious future channels that anger toward a goal. The potential effectiveness of this temporal strategy can be seen from the fact that it helped persuade millions of Scottish voters to give their support to an independence referendum whose success might have resulted in a sharp drop in their own standard of living. Such extremist ideologies as Nazism have also made use of this temporal strategy. For the Nazis, such historical inventions as the "stab in the back" that allegedly produced Germany's defeat in World War I were designed to produce anger to be channeled toward the creation of a glorious future under Nazi leadership.

Candidate Donald Trump's 2016 "Make America Great Again" slogan was an echo of this strategy. Surveys indicated that millions of working-class White Americans were resentful because of a sense that their own prominence in America had declined relative to minorities and others.[11] Trump's slogan and campaign more generally were designed to appeal to these feelings of disenfranchisement and disempowerment. For Trump, the historical stab in the back consisted of the opening of America's borders to undocumented immigrants coupled with economic policies that led to the export of working-class jobs. This Trumpian history was designed to produce anger that could be directed toward a future goal—a restoration of American (read White American) greatness—and the election of Donald Trump. And Trump's reinvention of the past and future brought new voters to the polls and changed the voting behavior of significant numbers of White, blue-collar voters. This gave Trump an electoral victory that confounded poll predictions based upon established patterns of voting behavior. Through his reinterpretation of the past and future, Trump established a new political reality and undermined previously accepted "alternative facts," as his administration called them.

Perhaps such examples are not as dramatic as the use of time travel in

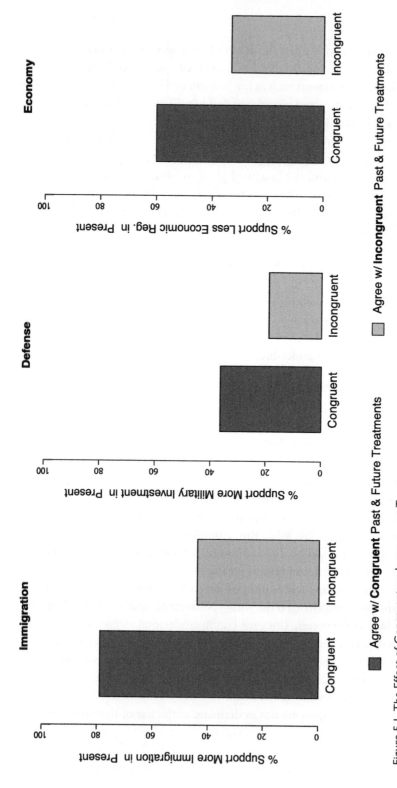

Figure 5.1. The Effect of Congruent vs. Incongruent Treatments

These bar plots show the reinforcing effect of historical and future frames. Those who received reinforcing frames were more likely to support the present-day policy position that aligned with these frames. Those who received incongruous frames, in contrast, were less likely to support this same policy position.

films like *The Terminator*. Yet these manipulations of time show that those able to influence what people believe about the past and future can exercise considerable influence in the present as well. No one can send lethal weapons from the future to do battle in the present. Contending political forces can, however, develop ideas about the future to materialize in the present where, if wanted, lethal weapons can be produced. Was *The Terminator* truly a work of fiction?

Of course, the revised past and reimagined future are no more carved in stone than the ideas they displaced. What one set of political forces invents or imagines can be reinvented or reimagined still again by competing forces and must constantly be defended against such efforts. Past, present, and future are always products of a political struggle in which those who have invented a new narrative are anxious to maintain control of the story and to prevent even a whisper of the old narrative.

We can see quantitatively that historical narrative is reinforced by repetition and undermined by contradiction. During the course of our study, some respondents received "reinforcing" prompts, that is, they were given history lessons followed by future forecasts confirming the history lessons (we saw this in chapter 4), while other respondents were given contradictory prompts, that is, history lessons followed by future forecasts contradicting the history lessons. Figure 5.1 compares the result of reinforcing versus contradictory prompts in three issue domains.

For example, among respondents who agreed with both the historical and future treatments that framed immigration in a positive manner, 79 percent expressed support for increasing immigration in the present day. Among those who were presented with contradictory statements about immigration (e.g., a positive historical frame and a negative future frame), only 44 percent expressed support for increasing immigration today. A similar effect is evident with respect to the economy. Among those who agreed with both a historical and future treatment that framed business regulations as bad for the economy, 60 percent expressed support for reducing private-sector regulations today. Among those who were presented with contradictory statements about the impact of business regulations, only 33 percent expressed support for reducing these regulations today. In the political world, contending forces battle to reinforce historical perspectives they favor or undermine histories they discountenance. History is always unsettled—a matter for ongoing debate and struggle.

We conclude with the observation that the idea of a fixed past and a tomorrow that follows in some orderly way from today is little more than an illusion. To some, this idea may be disquieting, replacing a comfortable reality with unease and uncertainty. Others may find the idea of a malleable reality exhilarating and empowering. For better or worse, humans exercise a measure of control over reality—it is not simply imposed upon them.

In the case of temporal reality, a good deal of this control is exercised through the mechanism of political struggle. Competing political forces work to invent and reinvent the past and future and, thereby, to control the present to their own advantage. Temporal reality is constituted in the political arena.

Appendix

National Survey on Policy Attitudes

The survey was administered to a nationally representative sample of 1,814 respondents in May 2017. The survey was built using Qualtrics software and Qualtrics administered the survey online to a sample that is representative of the U.S. with respect to age, race and gender (based on Census proportions).

Part I: Demographic Information

Are you male or female?

○ Male
○ Female

Which category below includes your age?

○ 18–20
○ 21–24
○ 25–34
○ 35–44
○ 45–54
○ 55–64
○ 65 and older

Information about income is very important to understand. Would you please give your best guess? Please indicate the answer that includes your entire household income in (previous year) before taxes.

- O Less than $10,000
- O $10,000 to $19,999
- O $20,000 to $29,999
- O $30,000 to $39,999
- O $40,000 to $49,999
- O $50,000 to $59,999
- O $60,000 to $69,999
- O $70,000 to $79,999
- O $80,000 to $89,999
- O $90,000 to $99,999
- O $100,000 to $149,999
- O $150,000 or more

What is the highest level of school you have completed or the highest degree you have received?

- O Less than high school degree
- O High school graduate (high school diploma or equivalent including GED)
- O Some college but no degree
- O Associate degree in college (2-year)
- O Bachelor's degree in college (4-year)
- O Master's degree
- O Doctoral degree
- O Professional degree (JD, MD)

Thinking about politics these days, how would you describe your own political viewpoint?

- O Very liberal
- O Liberal
- O Moderate
- O Conservative
- O Very conservative

Choose one or more races that you consider yourself to be:

○ White
○ Black or African American
○ American Indian or Alaska Native
○ Asian
○ Native Hawaiian or Pacific Islander
○ Other _____

Are you Spanish, Hispanic, or Latino or none of these?

○ Yes
○ None of these

Do you follow what's going on in government and public affairs?

○ Most of the time
○ Some of the time
○ Only now and then
○ Hardly at all

Part 2: Framing the Past

How much have you thought about the issue of crime?

○ A lot
○ A moderate amount
○ A little
○ Not at all

[Crime Treatment 1] As you may know, crime rates fell between the 1980s and 2010. Do you agree or disagree with the following? An important cause of the drop in crime rates was the adoption of "get tough" policies including longer prison terms.

○ Strongly agree
○ Agree

○ Disagree
○ Strongly disagree

[Crime Treatment 2] As you may know, crime rates fell between the 1980s and 2010. Do you agree or disagree with the following? An important cause of the drop in crime rates was making better education and social services available to potential offenders.

○ Strongly agree
○ Agree
○ Disagree
○ Strongly disagree

With crime rates on the rise in recent years, which of the following should be the primary focus of policymakers?

○ Strengthening mandatory minimum sentences
○ Investing in education and support services for at-risk youth

Have you held this view for a long time?

○ Yes
○ No

How much have you thought about the issue of immigration?

○ A lot
○ A moderate amount
○ A little
○ None at all

[Immigration Treatment 1] As you may know, millions of immigrants entered the U.S. illegally over the past two decades. Do you agree or disagree with the following statement? This history of illegal immigrants poses a threat to Americans' jobs, safety, and security.

○ Strongly agree
○ Agree
○ Disagree
○ Strongly disagree

[Immigration Treatment 2] As you may know, millions of immigrants entered the U.S. illegally over the past two decades. Do you agree or disagree with the following statement? Undocumented immigrants have generally worked hard and contributed to America's economic growth.

○ Strongly agree
○ Agree
○ Disagree
○ Strongly disagree

With illegal immigration a serious concern today, which of the following should be the primary focus of policymakers?

○ Investing in border security, such as border patrol agents and monitoring visa overstays
○ Helping undocumented immigrants become American citizens

Have you held this view for a long time?

○ Yes
○ No

How much have you thought about the issue of health care?

○ A lot
○ A moderate amount
○ A little
○ None at all

[Health Treatment 1] As you may know, insurance premiums have risen sharply in the past few years. Do you agree or disagree with the following statement? An important cause of rising insurance premiums is the increased cost of medical care, including the prices of drugs and services, over the past several decades.

○ Strongly agree
○ Agree
○ Disagree
○ Strongly disagree

[Health Treatment 2] As you may know, insurance premiums have risen sharply in the past few years. Do you agree or disagree with the following statement? An important cause of rising insurance premiums is America's fee-for-service model (medical providers are paid for every visit, test, and procedure).

- O Strongly agree
- O Agree
- O Disagree
- O Strongly disagree

To combat rising health insurance premiums, which of the following should be the primary focus of policymakers?

- O Develop an alternative payment model in which medical providers are compensated based on the quality of care delivered.
- O Negotiate with drug companies and medical providers to lower the costs of pharmaceuticals and services.

Have you held this view for a long time?

- O Yes
- O No

How much have you thought about the issue of violence in America?

- O A lot
- O A moderate amount
- O A little
- O None at all

[Violence Treatment 1] As you may know, there have been a number of serious acts of violence in the past few years. Do you agree or disagree with the following statement? An important cause of violence in America is the country's long-standing failure to provide adequate care for those who suffer from mental illness.

○ Strongly agree
○ Agree
○ Disagree
○ Strongly disagree

[Violence Treatment 2] As you may know, there have been a number of serious acts of violence in the past few years. Do you agree or disagree with the following statement? An important cause of violence in America is the country's history of weak laws that make it easy for dangerous people to acquire guns.

○ Strongly agree
○ Agree
○ Disagree
○ Strongly disagree

To combat violence in America, which of the following should be the primary focus of policymakers?

○ Pass laws to make it harder for potentially dangerous people to buy guns.
○ Invest in community mental health and substance abuse programs.

Have you held this view for a long time?

○ Yes
○ No

Part 3: Framing the Future

How much have you thought about the issue of climate change?

○ A lot
○ A moderate amount
○ A little
○ None at all

[Climate Treatment 1] As you may know, scientists have been examining the future of climate change. Do you agree or disagree with the following statement? Although climate change is important, Americans will face more pressing economic and social concerns over the next several years.

- ○ Strongly agree
- ○ Agree
- ○ Disagree
- ○ Strongly disagree

[Climate Treatment 2] As you may know, scientists have been examining the future of climate change. Do you agree or disagree with the following statement? Climate change will seriously threaten our nation's well-being over the next several years.

- ○ Strongly agree
- ○ Agree
- ○ Disagree
- ○ Strongly disagree

Today, how should policymakers prioritize climate change?

- ○ Climate change should be a top policy priority.
- ○ Economic and jobs-related policies should be prioritized over climate change.

Have you held this view for a long time?

- ○ Yes
- ○ No

How much have you thought about America's military power?

- ○ A lot
- ○ A moderate amount
- ○ A little
- ○ None at all

[Military Treatment 1] There's been a lot of discussion about America's military strength compared to that of other powerful nations. Do you agree or disagree with the following statement? In the foreseeable future, American will continue to have the most powerful military of any nation.

○ Strongly agree
○ Agree
○ Disagree
○ Strongly disagree

[Military Treatment 2] There's been a lot of discussion about America's military strength compared to that of other powerful nations. Do you agree or disagree with the following statement? In the foreseeable future, America's military strength will decline compared to that of other great powers, such as China.

○ Strongly agree
○ Agree
○ Disagree
○ Strongly disagree

Today, how should the U.S. government prioritize military spending?

○ The government should prioritize military spending above all else.
○ The government should spend a bit more on domestic issues, like healthcare and infrastructure, and a bit less on the military.

Have you held this view for a long time?

○ Yes
○ No

How much have you thought about America's economy?

○ A lot
○ A moderate amount
○ A little
○ None at all

[Economy Treatment 1] There's been a lot of discussion about the future of the U.S. economy. Do you agree or disagree with the following statement? Over the next decade, more and more small businesses will go under owing to burdensome regulations.

- O Strongly agree
- O Agree
- O Disagree
- O Strongly disagree

[Economy Treatment 2] There's been a lot of discussion about the future of the U.S. economy. Do you agree or disagree with the following statement? Over the next decade, more and more corporations will continue to move offshore.

- O Strongly agree
- O Agree
- O Disagree
- O Strongly disagree

To help spur job growth today, which of the following should be a primary focus for policymakers?

- O Cutting corporate taxes to ensure American companies remain in the U.S.
- O Reducing business regulations that are costly to small businesses

Have you held this view for a long time?

- O Yes
- O No

How much have you thought about America's national debt?

- O A lot
- O A moderate amount
- O A little
- O None at all

[Debt Treatment 1] There's been a lot of discussion about controlling the national debt. Do you agree or disagree with the following statement? America's debt is enormous and will be a severe burden on today's children.

- ○ Strongly agree
- ○ Agree
- ○ Disagree
- ○ Strongly disagree

[Debt Treatment 2] There's been a lot of discussion about controlling the national debt. Do you agree or disagree with the following statement? When considered as a percentage of GDP, the national debt is not problematic and does not threaten the future economy.

- ○ Strongly agree
- ○ Agree
- ○ Disagree
- ○ Strongly disagree

Today, how should policymakers approach spending?

- ○ Cut entitlement programs to rein in the national debt
- ○ Maintain current spending levels on social programs and other national priorities

Have you held this view for a long time?

- ○ Yes
- ○ No

Part 4: Framing the Future and the Past

[Immigration Treatment 1 Subgroup A] Do you agree or disagree with the following statement? Implementing thoughtful immigration restrictions will make America a better country.

- ○ Strongly agree
- ○ Agree
- ○ Disagree
- ○ Strongly disagree

[Immigration Treatment 2 Subgroup A] Do you agree or disagree with the following statement? America was better off prior to the recent wave of immigration.

- ○ Strongly agree
- ○ Agree
- ○ Disagree
- ○ Strongly disagree

[Immigration Treatment 1 Subgroup B] Do you agree or disagree with the following statement? Restricting immigration will make America worse off.

- ○ Strongly agree
- ○ Agree
- ○ Disagree
- ○ Strongly disagree

[Immigration Treatment 2 Subgroup B] Do you agree or disagree with the following statement? America was worse off prior to the recent wave of immigration.

- ○ Strongly agree
- ○ Agree
- ○ Disagree
- ○ Strongly disagree

Today, should policymakers be encouraging immigration or restricting immigration?

- ○ Encouraging immigration
- ○ Restricting immigration

Have you held this view for a long time?

- ○ Yes
- ○ No

How much have you thought about the issue of war and peace?

- ○ A lot
- ○ A moderate amount
- ○ A little
- ○ None at all

[War and Peace Treatment 1 Subgroup A] Do you agree or disagree with the following statement? The U.S. will be safer if it increases its military strength in the coming decades.

- ○ Strongly agree
- ○ Agree
- ○ Disagree
- ○ Strongly disagree

[War and Peace Treatment 2 Subgroup A] Do you agree or disagree with the following statement? Historically, the U.S. was safest when it was militarily most powerful.

- ○ Strongly agree
- ○ Agree
- ○ Disagree
- ○ Strongly disagree

[War and Peace Treatment 1 Subgroup B] Do you agree or disagree with the following statement? The U.S. will be safer if it works to promote international cooperation and disarmament in the coming decades.

- ○ Strongly agree
- ○ Agree
- ○ Disagree
- ○ Strongly disagree

[War and Peace Treatment 2 Subgroup B] Do you agree or disagree with the following statement? Historically, the U.S. was safest when it avoided conflicts with other nations.

- ○ Strongly agree
- ○ Agree
- ○ Disagree
- ○ Strongly disagree

Today, what should be the government's priority?

- ○ Investing more in the military
- ○ Working more with international organizations to resolve conflicts peacefully

Have you held this view for a long time?

- ○ Yes
- ○ No

[Economy Treatment 1 Subgroup A] Do you agree or disagree with the following statement? Over the next century, nations whose governments stop trying to regulate their economies and leave more economic decisions to the private sector will be better off.

- ○ Strongly agree
- ○ Agree
- ○ Disagree
- ○ Strongly disagree

[Economy Treatment 2 Subgroup A] Do you agree or disagree with the following statement? Historically, the U.S. was better off when the government stayed out of economic matters.

- ○ Strongly agree
- ○ Agree
- ○ Disagree
- ○ Strongly disagree

[Economy Treatment 1 Subgroup B] Do you agree or disagree with the following statement? Over the next century, nations whose governments learn to successfully manage their economies will be better off.

- ○ Strongly agree
- ○ Agree
- ○ Disagree
- ○ Strongly disagree

[Economy Treatment 2 Subgroup B] Do you agree or disagree with the following statement? Historically, the U.S. was better off when the government intervened to improve the economy.

- ○ Strongly agree
- ○ Agree
- ○ Disagree
- ○ Strongly disagree

Today, what should be the government's priority?

- ○ Making stronger efforts to regulate economic matters
- ○ Leaving more economic decisions to the private sector

Have you held this view for a long time?

- ○ Yes
- ○ No

How much have you thought about American foreign policy?

- ○ A lot
- ○ A moderate amount
- ○ A little
- ○ None at all

[Foreign Policy Treatment 1 Subgroup A] Do you agree or disagree with the following statement? In the future, the greatest threat to American interests will come from China.

- ○ Strongly agree
- ○ Agree
- ○ Disagree
- ○ Strongly disagree

[Foreign Policy Treatment 2 Subgroup A] Do you agree or disagree with the following statement? Historically, the U.S. has had generally friendly relations with Russia.

- ○ Strongly agree
- ○ Agree
- ○ Disagree
- ○ Strongly disagree

[Foreign Policy Treatment 1 Subgroup B] Do you agree or disagree with the following statement? In the future, the greatest threat to American interests will come from Russia.

- ○ Strongly agree
- ○ Agree
- ○ Disagree
- ○ Strongly disagree

[Foreign Policy Treatment 2 Subgroup B] Do you agree or disagree with the following statement? Historically, the U.S. has had generally friendly relations with China.

    ○ Strongly agree
    ○ Agree
    ○ Disagree
    ○ Strongly disagree

Today, what should be the government's priority?

    ○ Improving relations with Russia to block Chinese power
    ○ Improving relations with China to block Russian power

Have you held this view for a long time?

    ○ Yes
    ○ No

How much have you thought about the problem of attacks against the U.S. by foreign terrorists?

    ○ A lot
    ○ A moderate amount
    ○ A little
    ○ None at all

[Foreign Terrorism Treatment 1 Subgroup A] Do you agree or disagree with the following statement? It is highly likely that within the next decade foreign terrorists will attack America.

    ○ Strongly agree
    ○ Agree
    ○ Disagree
    ○ Strongly disagree

[Foreign Terrorism Treatment 2 Subgroup B] Do you agree or disagree with the following statement? Historically, America's best defense against foreign terrorism was to strike the terrorists before they could attack us.

- ○ Strongly agree
- ○ Agree
- ○ Disagree
- ○ Strongly disagree

[Foreign Terrorism Treatment 2 Subgroup A] Do you agree or disagree with the following statement? Americans don't have that much to fear from foreign terrorists in the coming years.

- ○ Strongly agree
- ○ Agree
- ○ Disagree
- ○ Strongly disagree

[Foreign Terrorism Treatment 2 Subgroup B] Do you agree or disagree with the following statement? Historically, America has had less to fear from foreign terrorism when it maintained good relations with other nations.

- ○ Strongly agree
- ○ Agree
- ○ Disagree
- ○ Strongly disagree

Today, what should be our government's priority?

- ○ Use our military to destroy foreign terrorists before they can attack us
- ○ Use diplomacy and international organizations to solve the problems that can lead to terrorism

Have you held this view for a long time?

○ Yes
○ No

Notes

Preface

1. Elizabeth F. Cohen, *The Political Value of Time* (New York: Cambridge University Press, 2018). Also, Tim Stevens, "Governing the Time of the World," in *Time, Temporality and Global Politics*, ed. Andrew Hom, Christopher McIntosh, Alasdair McKay, and Liam Stockdale (Bristol, England: E-International Relations Publishing, 2016), 59–72. On the power of the clock, see Eugen Weber, *Peasants into Frenchmen: The Modernization of Rural France, 1870–1914* (Stanford: Stanford University Press, 1976).

2. Andrew Hom, "Silent Order: The Temporal Turn in Critical International Relations," *Millennium: Journal of International Studies* 46, no. 3 (June 2018): 1–48. https://doi.org/10.1177/0305829818771349

3. See Paul Ricoeur, *Memory, History, Forgetting* (Chicago: University of Chicago Press, 2004).

4. Norbert Elias, *An Essay on Time* (Dublin: University College Press, 2007). Also, Andrew R. Hom, "Timing Is Everything: Toward a Better Understanding of Time and International Politics," *International Studies Quarterly* 62, no. 1 (March 2018):69–79.

5. Karen Barad, *Meeting the Universe Halfway* (Durham: Duke University Press, 2007), chap. 5.

6. Maurice Halbwachs, *On Collective Memory*, ed. and trans. Lewis A. Coser (Chicago: University of Chicago Press, 1992).

7. Ronald R. Krebs, *Narrative and the Making of U.S. National Security* (New York: Cambridge University Press, 2015). Also, Robert Bates et al., *Analytic Narratives* (Princeton: Princeton University Press, 1998).

Chapter 1

1. Pierre Nora, *Realms of Memory: Rethinking the French Past*, ed. Lawrence Kritzman, trans. Arthur Goldhammer (New York: Columbia University Press, 1996), xvii.

2. https://www.nytimes.com/interactive/2019/08/14/magazine/1619-america-slavery.html

3. http://everythingforever.com/einstein.htm

4. Jeffrey Haydu. "Making Use of the Past: Time Periods as Cases to Compare and as Sequences of Problem Solving." *American Journal of Sociology* 104, no. 2 (1998): 339–71.

5. Robert Darnton, "A Buffet of French History," *New York Review of Books*, May 11, 2017, 40.

6. Howard French, *Everything under the Heavens: How the Past Helps Shape China's Push for Global Power* (New York: Knopf, 2017).

7. Timothy Snyder, "Poland, Lithuania and the Ukraine, 1939–1999," in *Memory and Power in Post-War Europe*, ed. Jan-Werner Muller (New York: Cambridge University Press, 2002), 41.

8. Cara Buckley, "Two Films Reflect an Old Struggle to Control History," *New York Times*, April 22, 2017, C1.

9. Jeremy Kuzmarov, "Ken Burns's Documentary Promotes Misleading History: Its First Episode Can Be Understood as a Sophisticated Exercise in Empire Denial," *HuffPost*, September 20, 2017. http://www.huffingtonpost.com/entry/burns-vietnam-documentary-promotes-misleading-history_us_59bf4922e4b0390a1564df2b

10. Robert Kargon, "Model and Analogy in Victorian Science: Maxwell's Critique of the French Physicists," *Journal of the History of Ideas* 30, no. 3 (July–September, 1969), 423–436.

11. Lawrence Sklar, "The Elusive Object of Desire: In Pursuit of the Kinetic Equations and the Second Law," in *Time's Arrows Today: Recent Physical and Philosophical Work on the Direction of Time*, ed. Steven F. Savitt (Cambridge: Cambridge University Press, 1995), 191–216. See also Jill North, "Time in Thermodynamics," in *The Oxford Handbook of Philosophy of Time*, ed. Craig Callender, (New York: Oxford University Press, 2011), 312–52.

12. Thomas Hobbes, *Leviathan* (New York: Collier Books, 1962), 24.

13. http://www.pbs.org/wnet/jimcrow/stories_events_birth.html

14. William Dunning, *Reconstruction: Political and Economic, 1865–1877* (New York: Harper, 1907).

15. Eric Foner, *Reconstruction: America's Unfinished Revolution* (New York: Harper, 1988), xxii.

16. Daniel Kahneman, *Thinking, Fast and Slow* (New York: Farrar, Straus and Giroux, 2011), 202.

17. Jill Lepore, *The Whites of Their Eyes: The Tea Party's Revolution and the Battle over American History* (Princeton: Princeton University Press, 2010).

18. John Keane, "More Theses on the Philosophy of History," in *Meaning and Context: Quentin Skinner and His Critics*, ed. James Tully (Cambridge, MA: Polity, 1988), 204.

19. Josh Chin, "Xi Enforces Party's Version of History," *Wall Street Journal*, August 2, 2016, A8.

20. Dave Itzkoff, "'Confederate' Poses a Test for HBO," *New York Times*, July 22, 2017, C1.

21. Steven Sheffrin, *Rational Expectations*, 2nd ed. (New York: Cambridge University Press, 1996).

22. Maurice Duverger, *Political Parties: Their Organization and Activity in the Modern State* (New York: Wiley, 1954).

23. Bertell Ollman, "The Utopian Vision of the Future (Then and Now): A Marxist Critique," *Monthly Review* 57, no.3 (July–August, 2005). http://monthlyreview.org/20 05/07/01/the-utopian-vision-of-the-future-then-and-now-a-marxist-critique/

24. Karl Marx and Friedrich Engels, *On the Paris Commune* (Moscow: Progress, 1975), 172.

25. Edward Bellamy, *Looking Backward: 2000–1887* (New York: Signet, 1960).

26. Michel Houellebecq, *Soumission*, English ed. (New York: Farrar, Straus and Giroux, 2015).

27. Ignatius Donnelly, *Caesar's Column* (Cambridge, MA: Harvard University Press, 1960 [1889]).

28. Robert H. Kargon et al., *World's Fairs on the Eve of War* (Pittsburgh: University of Pittsburgh Press, 2015).

29. Kargon, *World's Fairs*, 2.

30. Kargon, *World's Fairs*, 63.

31. Friedrich Engels, *The Origins of the Family, Private Property and the State*, English ed. (New York: International Publishers, 1930).

32. Eleanor Burke Leacock, "Introduction to Origin of the Family, Private Property and the State." http://www.marxistschool.org/classdocs/LeacockIntro.pdf

33. Kenneth Scott, "Mussolini and the Roman Empire," *Classical Journal* 27, no. 9 (June 1932): 645–57.

34. Aatish Taseer, "The Return of History," *NYTimes.com*, December 11, 2015. http://mobile.nytimes.com/2015/12/11/opinion/the-return-of-history.html?emc=ed it_th_20151211&nl=todaysheadlines&nlid=19707266&referer=

35. M. Joshua Mozersky, "Presentism," in *The Oxford Handbook of Philosophy of Time*, ed. Craig Callender (New York: Oxford University Press, 2011), 123–44.

36. Simon Saunders, "How Relativity Contradicts Presentism," in *Time, Reality and Experience*, ed. Craig Callender (London: Cambridge University Press, 2002), 277–92. Also, Theodore Sider, *Four Dimensionalism: An Ontology of Persistence and Time* (Oxford: Oxford University Press, 2002), 42–52.

37. Bridget Murray, "What Makes Time Travel Possible?," *American Psychological Association Monitor* 34, no. 9 (October 2003). http://www.apa.org/monitor/oct03/me ntal.aspx

38. Allen Bluedorn, *The Human Organization of Time* (Stanford: Stanford University Press, 2002), chap.5. See also Michael J. Beran et al., "Looking Ahead," *Journal of Comparative Psychology* 129, no. 2 (2015): 160–73.

39. Peter Forrest, "The Real but Dead Past," *Analysis* 64, no. 4 (2004): 358–62. For a good introduction to these topics, see L. Nathan Oaklander, *The Ontology of Time* (Buffalo, NY: Prometheus, 2004), and James Harrington, *Time: A Philosophical Introduction* (London: Bloomsbury Academic, 2015).

Chapter 2

1. Linda B. Miller, "America after the Cold War: Competing Visions?," *Review of International Studies* 24 (1998): 251–59.

2. Thomas Berger, "German Foreign-Policy Making Since 1945," in *Memory and Power in Post-War Europe*, ed. Jan-Werner Muller (New York: Cambridge University Press, 2002), 76–99.

3. Konrad H. Jarausch, "Living with Broken Memories," in *The Divided Past: Rewriting Post-War German History*, ed. Christoph Klessmann (Oxford, UK: Berg, 2001), 191.

4. Geoffrey W. Conrad and Arthur A. Demarest, *Religion and Empire* (Cambridge: Cambridge University Press, 1984), 186.

5. Eugen Weber, *Peasants into Frenchmen* (Stanford: Stanford University Press, 1976), chap. 6.

6. J. Arch Getty, *Yezhov: The Rise of Stalin's Iron Fist* (New Haven: Yale University Press, 2008).

7. Chad O'Carroll, "Is North Korea Now Erasing History?," *Telegraph*, December 16, 2013. http://www.telegraph.co.uk/news/worldnews/asia/northkorea/10520935/Is -North-Korea-now-erasing-history.html

8. Gary Cutting, "Learning History at the Movies," *New York Times*, November 29, 2012. http://opinionator.blogs.nytimes.com/2012/11/29/learning-history-at-the -movies/?_r=0

9. Robert Burgoyne, *The Hollywood Historical Film* (Malden, MA: Blackwell, 2008), 8.

10. James Chapman, *Past and Present: National Identity and the British Historical Film* (London: I.B. Tauris, 2005), 94.

11. Jay Leyda. *Kino: A History of the Russian and Soviet Film*, 3ed ed. (Princeton: Princeton University Press, 1983), 348–50.

12. J. E. Smythe, *Reconstructing American Historical Cinema* (Lexington: University Press of Kentucky, 2006), 311.

13. Clayton R. Koppes and Gregory D. Black, *Hollywood Goes to War: How Politics, Profits, and Propaganda Shaped World War II Movies* (Berkeley: University of California Press, 1990), 22.

14. Koppes and Black, *Hollywood Goes to War*, 23.

15. Koppes and Black, *Hollywood Goes to War*, 27.

16. Susan A. Brewer, *Why America Fights: Patriotism and War Propaganda from the Philippines to Iraq* (New York: Oxford University Press, 2009), 92.

17. Clayton R. Koppes and Gregory D. Black, *Hollywood Goes to War: How Politics, Profits and Propaganda Shaped World War II Movies* (Berkeley: University of California Press, 1987).

18. https://www.rottentomatoes.com/m/1015260_north_star

19. Jonathan Zimmerman, *Whose America? Culture Wars in the Public Schools* (Cambridge, MA: Harvard University Press, 2002), 22–25.

20. Cameron McWhirter, "Textbooks on Islam Spark Controversy," *Wall Street Journal*, January 16, 2016, A3.

21. Joseph Moreau, *Schoolbook Nation: Conflicts over American History Textbooks from the Civil War to the Present* (Ann Arbor: University of Michigan Press, 2003).

22. Laura Isensee, National Public Radio, *All Things Considered*, "How Textbooks Can Teach Different Versions of History," July 13, 2015. http://www.npr.org/sections /ed/2015/07/13/421744763/how-textbooks-can-teach-different-versions-of-history

23. Reinhard Muller, *Deutschland: Sechster Teil* (Munich: R. Oldenbourg Verlag, 1943). Translated in Calvin College German Propaganda Archive. http://research.calv in.edu/german-propaganda-archive/textbk02.htm

24. Fritz Stern, *Gold and Iron: Bismarck, Bleichroder, and the Building of the German Empire* (New York: Vintage, 1977).

25. Mary Mills, "Propaganda and Children during the Hitler Years," https:// www.jewishvirtuallibrary.org/jsource/Holocaust/propchil.html

26. Sean Goodell, "Cinema as Propaganda during the Third Reich," *Utah Historical Review* 2 (2012). http://epubs.utah.edu/index.php/historia/article/viewArticle/627

27. Selma Stern, *The Court Jew* (New Brunswick, NJ: Transaction, 1985).

28. Andreas Dorpalen, "Weimar Republic and Nazi Era in East German Perspective," *Central European History* 11, no. 3 (1978): 222.

29. Jeffrey Herf, *Divided Memory: The Nazi Past in the Two Germanys* (Cambridge, MA: Harvard University Press, 1997), 3.

30. Robert Shandley, *Rubble Films* (Philadelphia: Temple University Press, 2001).

31. Omer Bartov, "Celluloid Soldiers: Cinematic Images of the Wehrmacht," in *Russia: War, Peace and Diplomacy*, ed. Ljubica Erickson and Mark Erickson (London: Weidenfeld and Nicolson, 2004), 130–43.

32. Julian Dierkes, "The Trajectory of Reconciliation through History Education in Postunification Germany," in *Teaching the Violent Past: History Education and Reconciliation*, ed. Elizabeth A. Cole (Lanham, MD: Rowman & Littlefield, 2007), 36.

33. Jeffrey Herf, *Divided Memory: The Nazi Past in the Two Germanys* (Cambridge, MA: Harvard University Press, 1997), 217.

34. Konrad J. Jarausch, "Living with Broken Memories," in *The Divided Past: Rewriting Post-War German History*, ed. Christoph Klessmann (New York: Oxford, 2001), 171–98.

35. Yasemin Nuhoglu Soysal, "Identity and Transnationalization in German School Textbooks," in *Censoring History: Citizenship and Memory in Japan, Germany, and the United States*, ed. Laura Hein and Mark Selden (Armonk, NY: M.E. Sharpe, 2000), 127–49.

36. Anton Troianovsky, "German Right Takes Aim at Wartime Guilt," *Wall Street Journal*, March 3, 2017, 1.

37. Alan S. Milward, "The Economic and Strategic Effectiveness of Resistance," in *Resistance in Europe, 1939–1945*, ed. Stephen Hawes and Ralph White (London: Allen Lane, 1975), 197.

38. Eric Conan and Henry Rousso, *Vichy: An Ever-Present Past* (Hanover, NH: University Press of New England, 1998).

39. "Russia's Past: The Rewriting of History," *Economist*, November 8, 2007. http:// www.economist.com/node/10102921

40. This said, we used regression analyses where possible to ensure the effects uncovered in cross tabulations are not being driven by any differences in demographics.

41. Andreas Hinz, Dominik Michalski, Reinhold Schwartz, and Philipp Yorck Hertzberg, "The Acquiescence Effect in Responding to a Questionnaire," *Psycho-social Medicine* 4, no. 7 (2007). https://www.ncbi.nlm.nih.gov/pmc/articles/PMC2736523/

42. In this case, the difference in means between the two groups has a p-value of 0.005.

43. Daniel Kahneman, *Thinking, Fast and Slow* (New York: Farrar, Straus and Giroux, 2011), 202. See also Richard E. Nisbett and Timothy D. Wilson, "Telling More Than We Can Know: Verbal Reports on Mental Processes." *Psychological Review* 84, no. 3 (1977).

44. These effects were obtained via an OLS regression analysis in which agreement with the history lesson was the dependent variable. The models controlled for political ideology, education, political engagement, income, race, age, and gender.

Chapter 3

1. Jeffrey A. Barrett, *The Quantum Mechanics of Minds and Worlds* (New York: Oxford University Press, 2001).

2. For a useful review of this literature, see Fabio Milani, "The Modeling of Expectations in Empirical DSGE Models: A Survey," http://www.economics.uci.edu/files/docs/workingpapers/2012-13/milani-01.pdf

3. Donald B. Redford, *A Study of the Biblical Story of Joseph* (Leiden, Netherlands: Brill, 1970).

4. Sun Tzu, *The Art of War*, chap. 2.

5. Niccolo Machiavelli, *The Art of War* (New York: Da Capo Press, 1965), 13.

6. Mike Konczal, "Buying the Future," *New Inquiry*, April 3, 2014. http://thenew inquiry.com/essays/buying-the-future/

7. Federal Insurance Office, U.S. Department of the Treasury, "Annual Report on the Insurance Industry," 2013. https://www.treasury.gov/initiatives/fio/reports-and -notices/Documents/FIO%20Annual%20Report%202013.pdf

8. Isaac Ehrlich and Jimyoung Kim, "Has Social Security Influenced Family Formation in OECD Countries? An Economic and Econometric Analysis," *National Bureau of Economic Research Working Papers*, no. 12869, January 2007. http://www.nb er.org/papers/w12869

9. Thomas Hobbes, *Leviathan*, ed. Ian Shapiro (New Haven: Yale University Press, 2010).

10. Immanuel Kant, "Perpetual Peace: A Philosophical Sketch." http://www.mtholy oke.edu/acad/intrel/kant/kant1.htm

11. Richard W. Fox, "Liberal Protestantism," in *A Companion to American Political Thought*, ed. Richard W. Fox and James T. Kloppenberg (Cambridge, MA: Blackwell, 1995), 394.

12. George M. Marsden, *Fundamentalism and American Culture* (New York: Oxford, 2006), 239.

13. Sydney Ahlstrom, *A Religious History of the American People* (New Haven: Yale University Press, 1972), 1099.

14. Michal B. Friedland, *Lift Up Your Voice Like a Trumpet: White Clergy and the Civil Rights and Antiwar Movements, 1954–73* (Chapel Hill: University of North Carolina Press, 1998).

15. George Marsden, *Fundamentalism and American Culture* (New York: Oxford, 2006), 238.

16. Timothy P. Weber, *On the Road to Armageddon: How Evangelicals Became Israel's Best Friend* (Grand Rapids, MI: Baker Publishing, 2004), 26.

17. Stephen Spector, *Evangelicals and Israel* (New York: Oxford, 2009), 15.

18. Spector, 14.

19. Timothy P. Weber, *On the Road to Armageddon: How Evangelicals Became Israel's Best Friend* (Grand Rapids, MI: Baker Publishing, 2004), 33.

20. Weber, *On the Road to Armageddon*, 36.

21. Weber, *On the Road to Armageddon*, 35.

22. The survey is representative with respect to age, race, and gender (based on census proportions).

23. Andreas Hinz, Dominik Michalski, Reinhold Schwartz, and Philipp Yorck Hertzberg, "The Acquiescence Effect in Responding to a Questionnaire," *Psycho-social Medicine* 4, no. 7 (2007). https://www.ncbi.nlm.nih.gov/pmc/articles/PMC2736523/

24. https://www.thenation.com/article/climate-denialism-is-literally-killing-us/. Marc Hertsgaard, "Climate Denialism Is Literally Killing Us," *Nation*, September 6, 2017.

25. These effects were obtained via an OLS regression analysis in which agreement with the history lesson was the dependent variable. The models controlled for political ideology, education, political engagement, income, race, age, and gender.

Chapter 4

1. Aaron Gerow, "Consuming Asia, Consuming Japan: The New Neonationalist Revisionism in Japan," in *Censoring History: Citizenship and Memory in Japan, Germany, and the United States*, ed. Laura Hein and Mark Selden (Armonk, NY: M.E. Sharpe, 2000), 74–95.

2. Jeffrey Olick, *The Guilt of Nations* (New York: W.W. Norton, 2000).

3. Ilana R. Bet-El, "Unimagined Communities: The Power of Memory and the Conflict in the Former Yugoslavia," in *Memory and Power in Post-War Europe*, ed. Jan-Werner Muller (New York: Cambridge University Press, 2002), 206

4. Bet-El, "Unimagined Communities," 213.

5. Jonathan Stubbs, *Historical Film: A Critical Introduction* (New York: Bloomsbury, 2013).

6. Susan Tegel, *Nazis and the Cinema* (London: Continuum Books, 2007), 34.

7. Brian Taves, *The Romance of Adventure: The Genre of Historical Adventure Movies* (Jackson: University Press of Mississippi, 1993), 14.

8. Matthew Robson, "Myth and Memory in the Pursuit of Scottish Independence," *Politica Critica*, December 19, 2015. http://politicacritica.com/lea-en-ingles/myth-and-memory-in-the-pursuit-of-scottish-independence/

9. http://whatscotlandthinks.org/questions/forced-choice-national-identity-5#bar

10. Elie Kedourie, *Nationalism* (New York: Wiley, 1993).

11. James L. Gelvin, *The Palestinian Conflict* (New York: Cambridge, 2014)

12. Daniel Polisar, "What Ordinary Palestinians Think about Jews, Israel, and Violence," *Los Angeles Times*, November 10, 2015. http://www.latimes.com/opinion/op-ed/la-oe-polisar-palestinian-public-opinion-20151112-story.html

Chapter 5

1. Helvi Inotila Elago, "Colonial Monuments in a Post-Colonial Era," in *Reviewing Resistance in Namibian History*, ed. Jeremy Silvester (Windhoek: University of Namibia Press, 2015), 276–91.

2. Karl Popper, *The Open Society and Its Enemies* (London: Routledge, 1945).

3. Alexander Wendt, "Anarchy Is What States Make of It: The Social Construction of Power Politics," *International Organization* 46, no. 2 (Spring 1992): 396–403.

4. Paul Davies and John Gribbin, *The Matter Myth* (New York: Simon & Schuster, 2007), chap. 1.

5. Jane Bennett, *Vibrant Matter* (Durham: Duke University Press, 2009).

6. Howard Schuman and Stanley Presser, *Questions and Answers in Attitude Surveys* (New York: Sage, 1981), 208.

7. Benjamin Ginsberg, *The Captive Public* (New York: Basic Books, 1986), chap. 3.

8. Robert Weissberg, *Polling, Policy and Public Opinion* (New York: Palgrave Macmillan, 2002).

9. Philip Mirowski, *Never Let a Serious Crisis Go to Waste* (London: Verso, 2013).

10. Fredric Jameson, *The Ideologies of Theory: Syntax of History* (Minneapolis: University of Minnesota Press, 1988), 154.

11. "American Rage: The Esquire/NBC News Survey," January 3, 2016. http://www.esquire.com/news-politics/a40693/american-rage-nbc-survey/

Index

Printed and bound by CPI Group (UK) Ltd, Croydon, CR0 4YY

09/06/2025

14686141-0005